Company's Coming ®

Grilling

INDOOR & OUTDOOR

Grilling

Second printing February 2000

Canadian Cataloguing in Publication Data
Jean Paré
 Grilling

Issued also in French under title:
Les grillades, à l'intérieur et à l'extérieur
Includes index.
At head of title: Company's Coming.
ISBN 1-896891-27-6

1. Barbecue cookery. 2. Broiling. I. Title.

TX687.P37 2000   641.7'6   C99-901367-X

Published simultaneously in Canada and the United States of America by The Recipe Factory Inc. in conjunction with Company's Coming Publishing Limited
2311 - 96 Street
Edmonton, Alberta, Canada
T6N 1G3
Tel: 780 • 450-6223
Fax: 780 • 450-1857
www.companyscoming.com

Company's Coming
COOKBOOKS®

Grilling was created thanks to the dedicated efforts of the people and organizations listed below.

COMPANY'S COMING PUBLISHING LIMITED

Chairperson
Jean Paré

President
Grant Lovig

V.P. Product Development
Kathy Knowles

Design
Jaclyn Draker
Denise Hodgins

Copywriting
Debbie Dixon

Typesetting
Marlene Crosbie

THE RECIPE FACTORY INC.

Research & Development Manager
Nora Prokop

Test Kitchen Supervisor
Lynda Elsenheimer

Project Assistant
Suzanne Hartman

Food Stylist
Carol MacLeod

Proofreader
Mimi Tindall

Photographer
Stephe Tate Photo

Prop Stylist
Frieda Lovig

Color separations, printing, and binding by Friesens, Altona, Manitoba, Canada
Printed in Canada

Our special thanks to the following businesses for providing extensive props for photography.

Artifacts
Club Monaco Everyday
Dansk Gifts
Le Gnome
Pacific Linen
Scona Clayworks
The Bay
Tile Town Ltd.
X/S Wares

FRONT COVER

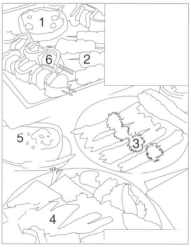

1. Italian Mushroom Grill, page 145
2. Exotic Pork Saté, page 111
3. Grilled Asparagus, page 146
4. Herbed Polenta And Chicken Salad, page 96
5. Chili Peanut Sauce, page 21
6. Scallop And Vegetable Skewers, page 113

Table of contents

Company's Coming
cookbooks

ASSORTED TITLES	
	Easy Entertaining (hardcover)
	Beef Today! (softcover)

LIFESTYLE SERIES	
	Grilling
	Low-fat Cooking
	Low-fat Pasta

KIDS TITLES	
	Kids - Lunches

COMPANY'S COMING SERIES

50 Delicious Squares	Light Recipes
Casseroles	Microwave Cooking
Muffins & More	Preserves
Salads	Light Casseroles
Appetizers	Chicken, Etc.
Desserts	Kids Cooking
Soups & Sandwiches	Fish & Seafood
Holiday Entertaining	Breads
Cookies	Meatless Cooking
Vegetables	Cooking for Two
Main Courses	Breakfasts & Brunches
Pasta	Slow Cooker Recipes
Cakes	Pizza!
Barbecues	One-Dish Meals
Dinners of the World	Starters
Lunches	Stir-Fry NEW, March 2000
Pies	

GREATEST HITS

Biscuits, Muffins & Loaves
Dips, Spreads & Dressings
Soups & Salads NEW, April 2000
Sandwiches & Wraps NEW, April 2000

SELECT SERIES

Sauces & Marinades	30-Minute Meals
Ground Beef	Make-Ahead Salads
Beans & Rice	No-Bake Desserts

foreword

Grilling (or barbecuing) dates back about 300,000 years when man first used charcoal or charred wood in cooking fires. A lot has changed since then with how we prepare meals, but the lure of an open fire, the taste of smoked food, and the fun of cooking in the great outdoors has kept grilling a popular activity.

Previously reserved for warm summer months, grilling has now been brought indoors thanks to new appliances and stove tops specifically designed for this cooking style. What was once offered up as traditional summer fare is now a year-round alternative to frying, roasting, broiling or baking. Grilling is certainly a reflection of today's more casual lifestyle, offering quick, simple and affordable recipes.

The recipes in GRILLING have been designed and tested to help make the most of your grill—indoor or outdoor. Although most recipes can be done on either the appliance or on the charcoal barbecue, we have indicated whether we used the indoor electric grill or the outdoor gas barbecue. As well, there is a specific Two-Sided Grilling section for recipes using the model of electric grill that has a hinged lid for full contact on both sides of the food. Some recipes requiring the indirect method of cooking (see page 7) must be done on the gas (or charcoal) barbecue and won't be interchangeable with the electric grill.

Best of all, these recipes are suitable for almost any occasion. Most recipes can be doubled or tripled but to help you with your next big barbecue party, browse through the Backyard Party section, pages 24 through 27. And there's more. In amongst these great recipes you'll find tips and suggestions on how best to prepare, cook and serve your food. Even if you are an experienced barbecuer, you may want to review the Basics of Grilling, pages 6 and 7, and Grilling and Food Safety Tips, pages 8 and 9.

Because of its simple and basic approach to cooking food, the art of grilling has endured for thousands of years with little change and remains a favorite cooking style around the world. Today it continues to grow in popularity as a year-round activity, providing innovative and easy ways to prepare food for busy lifestyles. But don't forget that grilling was, is, and will always be, the ideal way to enjoy those warm, lazy summer days. Get GRILLING!

each recipe

has been analyzed using the most updated version of the Canadian Nutrient file from Health and Welfare Canada, which is based upon the United States Department of Agriculture (USDA) Nutrient Data Base. These analyses have been done using the ingredients listed in each recipe, with the exception of those identified as "optional" or "garnish". We have also used the first ingredient listed whenever a second alternative is offered (such as "butter or hard margarine"). If a range of servings is offered in a recipe, we analyzed the first serving amount, which is the larger serving size.

Margaret Ng, B.Sc. (Hon), M.A.
Registered Dietician

Basics of Grilling

 rilling is a year-round activity that can be done indoors or outdoors—the choice is yours. While the art of grilling goes back thousands of years, the tools we use to grill food are constantly evolving to suit the needs of each passing generation. Today there is a mixture of traditional and modern grills on the market, all of which do a satisfactory job of grilling practically any food you could want. GRILLING focuses on the indoor countertop electric grill (several types) and the outdoor gas barbecue. As the popularity of indoor grilling grows, many households will have the advantage of using both methods.

Electric Indoor Grills

Electric grills are gaining in popularity each year and have greatly added to the enjoyment of apartment and condo dwellers. Being able to duplicate the speed, flavor and look of outdoor barbecuing without having to deal with weather conditions, confined space and the potential hazards of gas, is appealing to more and more cooks. There are a number of different models in stores, each with varying features. The more common are:

1. One side only with no variable temperature (just on - hot - and off) and no additional flat surface.

2. One side only with variable temperature and a flat "griddle" surface at the side for frying.

3. Hinged two-sided (food is grilled on both sides at the same time) but no variable temperature (just on - hot - and off) and no flat surface.

Indoor grills are best suited for smaller quantities of food as their cooking surface area is about one-third of an outdoor barbecue. As well, foods with sugar-based marinades are not advised because of the potential for smoke.

Outdoor Barbecues

Adventurous outdoor chefs have had a variety of cooking options available for a long time. From potatoes nestled in the smoldering wood fire to steaks sizzling under the lid of the gas barbecue they can pick and choose their most preferred (or feasible) method. There is even the possibility of using several at the same time. Here is a brief description of the two most common types of outdoor barbecues:

Charcoal Barbecue

The most popular style is the round kettle-style base that allows easy mounding of the briquettes for optimum lighting and heat concentration. The coals can be spread out once they are smoldering for Direct Heat Cooking, page 7, or piled around the edges or to one side for Indirect Heat Cooking, page 7. Some models come with a lid to allow for roasting and smoking. Charcoal barbecues are less expensive than gas barbecues and have fewer parts and ongoing maintenance, but heat distribution is unpredictable, the cooled ash is messy to clean out, and it takes some time for the coals to get hot and glowing. The hibachi is the smallest and most portable in size of the charcoal-style barbecues.

Gas Barbecue

A gas barbecue offers the convenience of quick and even heat, and can be adjusted to cook at any temperature at any time. Instead of charcoal, propane or natural gas heats up lava rocks or ceramic briquettes, which in turn do a quick and efficient job of radiating heat.

Cooking Methods

Direct Heat Cooking: Food is cooked directly over the heat source. This method cooks the food quickly (under 30 minutes) and is best suited to smaller cuts of meat and poultry (steak, kabobs, burgers, vegetables and boneless chicken breasts). Choose this method for searing more tender cuts of meat on high, then lowering the heat setting or spreading coals out, to finish the cooking.

Indirect Heat Cooking: This option will work only with charcoal or gas barbecues that have a lid. The heat source is around the food rather than directly under it. With a charcoal barbecue, move the hot coals to the outer edges and either place the food on the grill above the open center or place it in a foil or metal pan directly in the center with the hot coals around it. Close the lid to cook. With a gas barbecue, turn off either the left or center burner after preheating. Place the food over the burner that has been turned off. Place a drip pan (see Tip, page 151) under the food, and close the lid. This is a slower process and works for roasts, ribs, and other larger, less tender cuts of meat. It also requires much less turning.

Grilling Tips

Grilling offers a distinctive and savory approach to preparing cooked food. That means you have all kinds of opportunities to get truly creative with your barbecue or electric grill. What follows are a few suggestions to help you get grilling:

• Preheat the grill. Use a high heat to preheat, then lower temperature to cook. Cooking on a cold grill will cause food to stick.

• Keep the lid closed whenever possible to allow both the smoke to envelop the food and the heat to stay constant.

• Cooking times for vegetables can vary: soft vegetables such as tomatoes take very little time to cook, while potatoes, beets and other hard vegetables may need to be blanched or boiled before grilling to cut down on cooking time. If you are mixing vegetables together in a packet or on a kabob, select those with similar firmness so that the contents cook evenly.

• Be aware that broiling/grilling times can vary for all foods, depending on the temperature of the barbecue, how high the grill is set from the coals, and the cut of meat.

• If a flare-up occurs, move food to one side until flames die down. Serious flare-ups can be quenched with baking soda, but don't use water on gas barbecues.

• If you are heating bread, offer double protection against direct heat by using two baking sheets.

Glossary of Grilling

Baste: To brush or dab food with a liquid such as a marinade, sauce or butter to help keep food moist, to add flavor, or to make an attractive glaze on the surface of the food.

Blanch (par-boil): To partially cook food, usually a vegetable, by immersing in boiling water for a few seconds to several minutes. Some vegetables need to be blanched prior to grilling to ensure they will be thoroughly cooked without burning.

Briquettes: Charcoal fuel that has been compacted into small uniformly shaped "bricks." Some brands include a flammable additive to make quick work of lighting and burning briquettes.

Brochettes: This is the French word for "skewer."

Butterfly: To split a solid piece of meat, such as a boneless chicken breast, pork tenderloin, and even large shrimp, horizontally down the center almost but not all the way through. The two halves open out to resemble a butterfly. This provides a more even thickness for grilling.

Glaze: To coat food with a thin glossy mixture by basting or brushing it on during that last 5 minutes or so of cooking time. The coating usually contains a sugar (granulated, brown, corn syrup, etc.) so the food should be watched carefully to avoid burning.

Grill Rack/Grate: A metal grid that sits suspended over the heat source and on which food is placed.

Kabob: Originally from the Middle East, these are bite-size pieces of food pushed onto a long wooden or metal stick and cooked by grilling or broiling. Also called "skewers" today.

Marinade: A seasoned liquid such as wine, vinegar and oil, in which food is soaked for a period of time to absorb flavors and in some cases, to tenderize.

Saté: Originating from Indonesia, these are small skewers of meat, poultry or seafood, marinated in a savory spicy sauce. Saté is often cooked on the shorter skewers and served as an appetizer.

Skewer: A thin metal or wooden stick that is used to hold pieces of meat, poultry, seafood or vegetables. Wooden skewers should be soaked for 10 minutes before placing on the grill.

Skewers: The more traditional name for skewers is kabobs (or kebabs) with "skewer" referring to the long pointed stick that the food is pierced or "skewered" with.

Truss: The process whereby a bird, such as a whole chicken, is tied up using heavy cotton or linen string to prevent wings and legs from falling loose. To best secure the bird, bend wing tips under the body then wrap and tie lengths of string around the center part of the legs, around the tips of the drumsticks, and the wings.

Grilling and Food Safety

Grilling Safety Tips

When using any cooking device, it's important that you maintain a level of caution to prevent unwanted accidents, burns and fires. This is especially true for charcoal and gas barbecues. Even if you are an experienced chef with the outdoor grill, you might want to take a moment to review these important safety tips.

Charcoal Barbecues

- Allow ashes to cool completely for at least 48 hours before disposing.

- Keep barbecue uncovered until ready to cook.

- Never use fuels not specifically designed for lighting charcoal.

- Never use lighter fluid on instant-start briquettes. Never add lighter fluid to hot coals.

- Never use an electric starter under wet weather conditions.

- Never move the barbecue while it is in use or hot.

- Keep vents open while cooking.

Gas Barbecues

• Always light the barbecue with the lid open.

• Always keep the barbecue in a well ventilated area, even when not in use.

• Always store cylinders in an upright, well ventilated and cool area.

• Always check for gas leaks immediately after reconnecting the cylinder to the barbecue. Put a little liquid dishwashing soap in a small cup with a bit of water. Using a basting brush, brush the soapy solution over places where you have reconnected. Watch for small bubbling indicating escaping gas.

• Always service your barbecue at least twice a year or after storage, looking for deterioration, burner obstruction, cracks in the hose, and damaged or aged O-rings. Use a soap and water solution to check for leaks.

• Always keep the grease drip tray at the bottom of the barbecue clean and free of debris, to avoid hazardous grease fires.

• Always shut both the burners and the gas off at their source after use.

• Never ask the propane dealer to overfill the cylinder, or to fill a cylinder that is damaged, dented or past its expiry date (cylinders are dated, and dealers should not refill cylinders older than 10 years).

• Never store a propane cylinder indoors, or in an area that exceeds 125°F (52°C).

• Never attach or disconnect a cylinder while the barbecue is hot.

• Never move the barbecue while it is in use or hot.

• Never operate the barbecue up against the side of the house.

• Never use water to extinguish flare-ups on a gas barbecue. Move the food to another part of the grill and wait until the flames die down.

Electric Grills

Safety precautions for electric grills are similar to those for any household appliance: Never use an electric grill in wet areas, or expose the grill and cords to water. Make certain the cord is properly grounded and in good condition, and keep the area clear around the grill while it is hot.

Food Safety Tips

Warm summer months may be a great time to fire up the barbecue, but it's also a tricky matter to make certain that food is prepared, cooked and served safely. Hot weather can turn perfectly good food into poison even on the car ride home from the grocery store. Always be aware of the temperature, and make sure that meat, dairy and poultry products are not exposed to heat for any length of time.

• Use only fresh meat, fish and poultry that have not been allowed to warm prior to cooking. At the grocery store, select these items last and check that packaging is not damaged.

• Transport food in a cool environment—an air-conditioned car, insulated cooler or ice-packed bags. Don't place groceries in the trunk of the car.

• Thaw frozen foods, particularly meat, fish and poultry in the refrigerator, not on the counter.

• Wash your hands thoroughly in hot, soapy water before handling any food.

• Keep raw meat and its juices away from other foods—use a separate cutting board and knife, and clean the board with a small quantity of chlorine bleach after use.

• Precook chicken or ribs immediately before grilling; do not allow the meat to cool down in between.

• Keep hot foods hot, and cold foods cold. Never leave food out in the sun. Wait until you are ready to eat before serving and then set them out in shady areas.

• Cook hamburger meat thoroughly until no pink shows through (see Tip, page 57).

• Marinate foods in the refrigerator, never on the counter. If you plan to use the marinade to baste your food, first bring it to a rolling boil for 10 minutes to kill any bacteria. If you are planning to serve the basting sauce, reheat to boiling for 10 minutes.

• Don't judge doneness of the meat by its color—it can be deceiving. Use an instant-read thermometer to ensure that the center of larger pieces of meat, fish and poultry are cooked.

Marinating Magic

To marinate means to create a savory acidic liquid that your meat, vegetables, poultry or seafood will stand or soak in for a period of time to tenderize and retain juiciness, as well as to enrich flavors. How much marinade you need depends on the amount of food to be marinated. A good guide is to plan on making about $^1/_2$ cup (125 mL) marinade for every 1 lb. (900 g) food. Marinade contains the majority of fat grams, so use only what's needed to coat and absorb for optimum flavor.

Key Ingredients

1. At least one acidic ingredient (such as vinegar, wine, lemon juice or other citrus fruit juice) partially helps to tenderize otherwise tough cuts of meat by breaking down the sinewy protein fibers. This process also encourages the absorption of marinade into the food.

2. An oil may or may not be added. While it adds moisture and helps to keep food from sticking to the grill during the cooking process, oil also adds fat grams so use cautiously.

3. A mixture of herbs, spices and other seasonings that enhance the flavor.

Note: Avoid adding salt to a marinade as it tends to dry out food.

To Marinate

1. Mix marinade ingredients in a nonmetallic pan—ceramic or glass works best. A plastic container also works fine but could possibly stain. A heavy-duty disposable plastic freezer bag may also be used and makes clean-up quick and easy. Regardless, the container should be large enough to lay meat or vegetables in a single layer, or to allow food to be stirred or turned.

2. Add the food and stir, or turn over, to coat thoroughly. Cover or seal tightly and place in the refrigerator. Stir or turn food occasionally during the suggested standing time. Tender cuts of meat, as well as poultry and fish and seafood, might require as little as 15 minutes to marinate; less tender steaks or roasts may need to marinate overnight.

3. Remove the food from the marinade, letting excess liquid drip back into the container. You may even want to blot the food with paper towel.

4. Place food on the preheated grill.

5. You have three choices with the remaining marinade: (1) discard immediately (this means you are throwing away some of the fat grams), (2) boil and use for basting the food during grilling, or (3) reheat to a rolling boil for 1 to 5 minutes after marinating or basting to kill any bacteria from the uncooked meat, and then serve as a sauce with the grilled food.

tip

If you are looking for a quick marinade, consider using a store-bought non-creamy salad dressing such as Italian.

Wood Chips and Other Aromatics

Adding mesquite, hickory, fruitwood or other aromatic wood chips to the gas or charcoal barbecue gives you that delicious wood-smoked flavor which makes grilled foods taste so unique.

Soak chips in water, then add directly to the hot coals of a charcoal barbecue. For a gas barbecue, poke small holes in a piece of heavy-duty aluminum foil or foil container. Lay the wet chips in a single layer on the foil or in the pan and place directly on the heat source. Preheat the barbecue and wait for smoke to appear before cooking. Close the lid to allow smoke to surround and permeate the food.

Dried herbs are another great aromatic. Select a combination of your favorite dried herbs, soak them in water, squeeze out excess moisture, and then add directly onto the hot coals or sprinkle in a foil pan and place directly on the heat source.

For a really quick aromatic, add citrus peel directly onto hot coals or put into foil pan and place directly on the heat source. Or try fresh rosemary branches placed directly on the heat source.

Tools and Accessories

For almost every task there are tools that we need to get the job done, and tools we'd like to have to make the job easier. The same holds true for grilling. Although indoor grilling can take advantage of the tools and accessories already available for oven and stove top cooking, outdoor grilling is a different matter. Here is a handy list of tools and equipment:

Outdoor Grilling Tools

Necessary:

Basting Brush: A sturdy, long-handled brush with natural bristles will make any basting job simple and quick.

Cleaning Brush: A proper rustproof wire brush specifically designed for barbecue grates will make quick work of an otherwise tedious and dirty task.

Long-Handled Utensils: The heat of an outdoor grill can become intense, making long-handled utensils invaluable tools to have. Tongs, spatulas and forks are all available in this style.

Oven Mitts: Padded, flame-resistant long oven mitts that reach almost to the elbow are highly recommended for use while barbecuing because of the danger of flare-ups.

Spray Bottle (water): Use a spritz of water to put out flare-ups in your charcoal barbecue. Water can also create moisture or smoke for your food. Never use water on a gas barbecue.

Outdoor Grilling Accessories

Wish list:

Apron: A bib-style apron helps to protect your clothing but also helps to designate the "official" in charge of the barbecue and grilling.

Chimney Starter: The unique design of this metallic cylindrical container allows you to get charcoal briquettes lit quickly using just a piece of newspaper.

Disposable Foil Pans: These are important if you do a lot of indirect grilling. Place directly under food to catch grease, or alternately, fill with water to impart moisture during cooking.

Grill Baskets: These baskets come in a variety of sizes and shapes according to their function. Long, narrower baskets can accommodate grilled fish, while wider baskets can be used to cook other delicate foods, vegetables, even stuffed pastas and pizza. Spray or brush the grill with cooking oil and heat for a minute before using. This will help to prevent food from sticking.

Electric Fire Starter: This kind of starter is used to heat charcoal briquettes and plugs into an outlet. The coiled end is an effective way to get charcoal lighted quickly.

Grill Thermometer: This thermometer is placed inside the barbecue to determine cooking temperature.

Grilling Nightlight or Flashlight: Truly a griller's delight! If you choose, there are fun gadgets specifically designed to hook onto the side of the barbecue, or a simple flashlight with a clamp or stand, that will help illuminate your meal and ensure a cooked dinner.

Instant-Read Thermometer: This thermometer is pushed into meat or poultry to test doneness, and offers an almost instant read of the temperature. This is an important tool to have when you are grilling larger cuts of meat or poultry, to make certain they have been cooked to the center.

Skewers: A set of skewers will give you the option of serving kabobs. Made of metal (stainless steel) or bamboo, skewers generally come in multiples and may or may not come with a complementary rack. Bamboo or wooden skewers must be soaked in water for about 10 minutes just before using to help prevent burning during cooking. Bamboo skewers come in several different lengths or they can be cut to preferred length. Metal skewers can be round, flat-sided, double-pronged, or even hoop-shaped.

Spare Gas Cylinder: An indulgence you may want to consider if you use your gas barbecue frequently throughout the warm weather months, or when entertaining large groups.

Spark Lighter: These lighters can be purchased and are long-handled, butane lighters that spark electronically to assist in lighting a gas barbecue.

Accompaniments

auces, salsas, butters and dips all enhance the flavor of grilled meats, poultry and seafood. The freshness of mango and papaya, bursts of flavor of red hot chilies and herbs, and the mellow taste of grilled peppers find their way into these recipes. There is even Barbecued Flatbread and cornmeal-based Grilled Johnny Cake. Lots of added touches to make your meal more interesting!

Blended Pepper Coulis

This puréed sauce carries the rich flavor of bell peppers but with a mild garlic taste and just a hint of sweetness. Serve with Basted Mini Salmon Rolls, page 69, or other grilled fish or chicken. Pictured on back cover.

Medium red peppers	2	2
Small garlic clove, minced	1	1
Green onion, chopped	1	1
Chopped fresh parsley	1 tbsp.	15 mL
Chopped fresh sweet basil	1 tbsp.	15 mL
Dry (or alcohol-free) white wine	2 tbsp.	30 mL
Granulated sugar	$1/2$ tsp.	2 mL
Salt	$1/4$ tsp.	1 mL
Freshly ground pepper, sprinkle		
Lemon juice	$1^1/2$ tsp.	7 mL

Preheat electric grill to high. Place whole red peppers on ungreased grill. Cook for 30 to 40 minutes, turning several times, until skins are blistered and black. Place in small bowl. Cover with plastic wrap. Allow to cool for 15 minutes. Peel skins off. Remove seeds and veins back into bowl along with any juices. Strain juices through sieve into blender. Put pepper pieces into blender. ■ Add remaining 9 ingredients. Process, using pulsing motion and scraping down sides, until mixture is puréed. Makes $1^3/4$ cups (425 mL).

2 tbsp. (30 mL): 5 Calories; trace Total Fat; 47 mg Sodium; trace Protein; 1 g Carbohydrate; trace Dietary Fiber

Sweet Grilled Salsa

Serve this warm or cold—wonderful flavor either way. A salsa without the sauce. Makes a very attractive and colorful presentation with grilled fish, chicken, beef or pork. Pictured on page 143.

Medium cobs of corn, husked	**3**	**3**
Boiling water, to cover		
Maple (or maple-flavored) syrup	**$^1/_3$ cup**	**75 mL**
Dried crushed chilies	**$^1/_4$ tsp.**	**1 mL**
Large red onion, cut into $^1/_2$ inch (12 mm) thick rings	**1**	**1**
Medium roma (plum) tomatoes, halved lengthwise and seeded	**3**	**3**
Medium zucchini, with peel, cut lengthwise into $^1/_4$ inch (6 mm) thick slices	**1**	**1**
Finely chopped fresh oregano leaves (or $^1/_2$ tsp., 2 mL, dried)	**2 tsp.**	**10 mL**
Finely chopped fresh sweet basil (or $^1/_2$ tsp., 2 mL, dried)	**2 tsp.**	**10 mL**
Salt	**$^1/_2$ tsp.**	**2 mL**
Pepper	**$^1/_4$ tsp.**	**1 mL**
Balsamic vinegar	**1-2 tbsp.**	**15-30 mL**

Preheat lightly sprayed electric grill to medium-high. Cook corn in boiling water in large saucepan or Dutch oven for 4 minutes. ■ Combine maple syrup and chilies in small bowl. Drain cobs. Place on grill. Baste with syrup mixture. Cook for about 8 minutes, turning frequently, until corn is golden and slightly charred. Cut kernels from cobs. Place kernels in medium bowl. ■ Place red onion rings, tomato slices and zucchini slices on greased grill. Baste with syrup mixture. Cook for 3 to 5 minutes, turning frequently, until soft and caramelized. Dice each slice. Add to corn kernels. ■ Season and toss with oregano, basil, salt, pepper and vinegar. Makes 4 cups (1 L).

2 tbsp. (30 mL): 21 Calories; 0.2 g Total Fat; 44 mg Sodium; trace Protein; 5 g Carbohydrate; 1 g Dietary Fiber

....

To peel a mango, slice through the flat side near the center, carving around the curve of the pit as you go. Repeat down the other side. Using a small sharp paring knife, score the flesh in small diamonds until the tip of the knife hits the skin but does not go through it. Using your hands and pressing on the skin side with thumbs, turn each section inside out, spreading the "diamonds" apart. Cut the pieces away from the skin.

Herb Aioli

Ay-OH-lee is a French sauce potent with garlic and the tang of homemade mayonnaise. Serve on grilled fish, chicken, lamb, or corn on the cob. Excellent with Middle East Pitas, page 51.

Garlic cloves, minced	3	3
Coarsely chopped fresh sweet basil	2 tbsp.	30 mL
Coarsely chopped fresh chives	1 tbsp.	15 mL
Coarsely chopped fresh parsley	1 tbsp.	15 mL
Salt	1 tsp.	5 mL
Freshly ground pepper, sprinkle		
Egg yolks (large)	2	2
Freshly squeezed lemon juice	1 tbsp.	15 mL
Grated lemon zest	$1/2$ tsp.	2 mL
Olive oil	$1/2$ cup	125 mL
Canola oil	$1/2$ cup	125 mL

Process first 9 ingredients in blender, scraping down sides as necessary to make smooth paste. ■ With motor running on high, slowly pour both oils in steady stream through opening in lid. Mixture should thicken into green, creamy mayonnaise-type sauce. Makes 1 cup (250 mL).

2 tsp. (10 mL): 86 Calories; 9.6 g Total Fat; 109 mg Sodium; trace Protein; trace Carbohydrate; trace Dietary Fiber

Cool Yogurt Dip

Excellent choice to serve with a platter of grilled vegetable chunks.

Thick (or strained) plain low-fat yogurt	1 cup	250 mL
Grated cucumber, with peel	$1/2$ cup	125 mL
Chopped fresh mint leaves, packed	2 tbsp.	30 mL
Salt	$1/4$-$1/2$ tsp.	1-2 mL
Granulated sugar	$1/4$ tsp.	1 mL

Combine all 5 ingredients in small bowl. Let stand at room temperature for 1 hour to meld flavors. Makes $1 1/3$ cups (325 mL).

1 tbsp. (15 mL): 8 Calories; 0.2 g Total Fat; 39 mg Sodium; 1 g Protein; 1 g Carbohydrate; trace Dietary Fiber

Mint Papaya Salsa

A great make-ahead for your next weekend barbecue bash. Keep a supply in the refrigerator for year-round indoor or outdoor grilling. Pictured on page 18.

Ripe medium papayas, peeled, seeded and diced	2	2
Finely diced red onion	1/2 cup	125 mL
Chopped fresh mint leaves	1/4 cup	60 mL
Lime juice	2 tsp.	10 mL
Salt	1/4 tsp.	1 mL
Freshly ground pepper, sprinkle		

Combine all 6 ingredients in small bowl. Cover. Let stand in refrigerator for at least 2 hours to meld flavors. Can be kept in refrigerator for up to 5 days. Makes 3 cups (750 mL).

2 tbsp. (30 mL): 11 Calories; trace Total Fat; 28 mg Sodium; trace Protein; 3 g Carbohydrate; trace Dietary Fiber

Fresh Mango Sauce

This smooth, thick sauce is delicious over grilled chicken breasts or pork.

Ripe large mango, flesh removed (see Tip, page 13)	1	1
Oyster sauce	1 tbsp.	15 mL
Dried crushed chilies	1/8 tsp.	0.5 mL
Small red hot chili pepper, seeds and veins removed (see Note)	1	1
Freshly squeezed lime juice	4 tsp.	20 mL
Finely grated lime peel	1/2 tsp.	2 mL
Granulated sugar	1 tbsp.	15 mL
Salt	1/4 tsp.	1 mL
Fresh cilantro, to taste (optional)	2 tbsp.	30 mL

Process all 9 ingredients in blender until smooth. Let stand for 1 hour to meld flavors. Makes 1 1/3 cups (325 mL).

1 tbsp. (15 mL): 10 Calories; trace Total Fat; 96 mg Sodium; trace Protein; 3 g Carbohydrate; trace Dietary Fiber

Note: When chopping hot peppers use gloves, as the caustic oily compounds, called capsaicin (kap-SAY-ih-sihn), permeate the skin and can cause a burning sensation.

Barbecued Flatbread

Brush the warm breads with oil and sprinkle with basil, oregano and Parmesan cheese— almost like a focaccia bread, but not quite.

All-purpose flour	2$^1/_2$ cups	625 mL
Whole wheat flour	$^1/_2$ cup	125 mL
Instant yeast	2$^1/_2$ tsp.	12 mL
Salt	1$^1/_2$ tsp.	7 mL
Granulated sugar	$^1/_4$ tsp.	1 mL
Freshly ground pepper, sprinkle		
Hot water (not boiling)	1 cup	250 mL
Italian dressing	2 tbsp.	30 mL

Process first 6 ingredients in food processor just to combine. ■ Combine hot water and dressing in small cup. Pour, in thin stream, through opening in lid while machine is running. Process, using pulsing motion, until mixture starts to form a ball. Turn out onto lightly floured surface. Knead until smooth and elastic. Place in greased bowl. Turn to grease top of dough. Cover with damp tea towel. Let stand in oven with light on and door closed for about 1 hour until doubled in bulk. Punch dough down. Cover. Let rest for 10 minutes. Divide dough into 8 equal pieces. Roll out or press into flat disc about $^1/_8$ inch (3 mm) thick. Cover with damp tea towel. Let stand for 30 minutes. Preheat barbecue to medium-low. Cook breads on greased grill for 2 to 3 minutes until bottom is spotted and bread is puffed. Turn with spatula. Cook for 2 to 3 minutes. Place cooked breads in covered container until cooled. They will deflate and soften as they cool. Makes 8 individual breads.

1 bread: 204 Calories; 3.1 g Total Fat; 569 mg Sodium; 6 g Protein; 38 g Carbohydrate; 3 g Dietary Fiber

Variation: After turning breads first time, brush cooked surface with olive oil and sprinkle with grated Parmesan cheese and dried sweet basil.

1. Sea Bass à la Caesar, page 132
2. Halibut With Mango Salsa, page 73

Grilled Johnny Cakes

We've suggested cutting the dough into rectangles, but any shape works. Serve for breakfast or brunch with jam or pancake syrup.

All-purpose flour	**1¼ cups**	**300 mL**
Yellow cornmeal	**¾ cup**	**175 mL**
Granulated sugar	**¼ cup**	**60 mL**
Baking powder	**1 tbsp.**	**15 mL**
Salt	**½ tsp.**	**2 mL**
Hard margarine (or butter)	**¼ cup**	**60 mL**
Large egg, fork-beaten	**1**	**1**
Milk	**¾ cup**	**175 mL**
All-purpose flour	**3 tbsp.**	**50 mL**

Preheat barbecue to medium-low. Combine first amount of flour, cornmeal, sugar, baking powder and salt in large bowl. Cut in margarine with pastry cutter until size of small peas. Make a well in center. ■ Whisk egg and milk together in small cup. Pour into well in dry ingredients. Stir together until flour is just moistened. Scrape dough out onto surface dusted with second amount of flour. Gently fold over 10 times, turning a quarter turn each time. Roll or pat out into ½ inch (12 mm) thickness. Cut into rectangles about 3 x 4 inches (7.5 x 10 cm). Place on greased grill. Close lid. Cook for 4 minutes per side. Makes 8 pieces.

1 piece: 243 Calories; 7.5 g Total Fat; 269 mg Sodium; 5 g Protein; 38 g Carbohydrate; 1 g Dietary Fiber

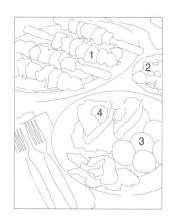

1. Souvlaki, page 122
2. Mint Papaya Salsa, page 15
3. Potatoes On A Stick, page 120
4. Rosemary Lamb Chops, page 85

Sesame Bread

This is ideally suited to the indoor grill. Serve to a hungry breakfast crew waiting at the table.

All-purpose flour	**1 cup**	**250 mL**
Whole wheat flour	**²/₃ cup**	**150 mL**
Sesame seeds	**¹/₄ cup**	**60 mL**
Baking powder	**4 tsp.**	**20 mL**
Granulated sugar	**2 tsp.**	**10 mL**
Salt	**1 tsp.**	**5 mL**
Canola oil	**6 tbsp.**	**100 mL**
Cold milk	**³/₄ cup**	**175 mL**
All-purpose flour, approximately	**¹/₄ cup**	**60 mL**

Preheat lightly sprayed electric grill to medium. Combine first 6 ingredients in large bowl. ■ Make a well in center. Pour in oil. Stir with fork until mixture is mealy. ■ Pour in cold milk. Stir with fork until just moistened. Turn out onto surface that has been sprinkled with 1 tbsp. (15 mL) flour. Knead, adding more flour, 1 tsp. (5 mL) at a time, until dough is not sticky. Divide in half. Pat out each portion to even thickness. Place on grill. Cook for 5 to 6 minutes per side. Cut each portion into 4, for a total of 8 pieces.

1 piece: 244 Calories; 13.2 g Total Fat; 362 mg Sodium; 5 g Protein; 27 g Carbohydrate; 2 g Dietary Fiber

Japanese Ginger Sauce

Serve on rice, or as a dipping sauce with Japanese Grilled Beef, page 28, or any grilled meat. Pictured on page 54.

Chopped preserved ginger, with liquid	**¹/₄ cup**	**60 mL**
Finely grated gingerroot	**1 tbsp.**	**15 mL**
Rice vinegar	**2 tbsp.**	**30 mL**
Low-sodium soy sauce	**2 tbsp.**	**30 mL**
Sesame oil	**1 tbsp.**	**15 mL**

Process all 5 ingredients in blender until not quite smooth. Makes ¹/₂ cup (125 mL).

1 tbsp. (15 mL): 27 Calories; 1.7 g Total Fat; 151 mg Sodium; trace Protein; 3 g Carbohydrate; trace Dietary Fiber

Chili Peanut Sauce

Peanut butter with a kick and a bite! Makes an excellent dipping sauce for Tandoori Chicken Sticks, page 105, or Exotic Pork Saté, page 111. Pictured on front cover.

Garlic clove, minced	**1**	**1**
Crunchy peanut butter	**$^1/_3$ cup**	**75 mL**
Low-sodium soy sauce	**2 tbsp.**	**30 mL**
Brown sugar, packed	**$1^1/_2$ tbsp.**	**25 mL**
Lemon juice	**1 tbsp.**	**15 mL**
Dried crushed chilies	**$^1/_4$ tsp.**	**1 mL**
Chili powder	**$^1/_4$ tsp.**	**1 mL**
All-purpose flour	**1 tbsp.**	**15 mL**
Skim evaporated milk	**1 cup**	**250 mL**

Combine first 7 ingredients in small saucepan. Heat over medium, stirring constantly, until liquid is well blended. ■ Whisk flour into evaporated milk in small bowl. Slowly add to brown sugar mixture, whisking constantly, until well blended and simmering. Will thicken slightly. Serve warm or cold. Makes 1$^1/_4$ cups (300 mL).

2 tsp. (10 mL): 30 Calories; 1.5 g Total Fat; 67 mg Sodium; 2 g Protein; 3 g Carbohydrate; trace Dietary Fiber

Seafood Butter

Wonderful on grilled fish of any kind, or with skewered seafood.

Unsalted butter, softened (about 4 oz., 113 g)	**$^1/_2$ cup**	**125 mL**
Chopped fresh parsley	**2 tbsp.**	**30 mL**
Freshly squeezed lemon juice	**1 tbsp.**	**15 mL**
Finely grated lemon peel	**1 tbsp.**	**15 mL**
Salt	**$^1/_2$ tsp.**	**2 mL**
Freshly ground pepper, sprinkle		

Whip butter with beaters in small bowl until light in color. ■ Beat in remaining 5 ingredients. Cover. Chill for 1 hour until butter can be formed into log about 6 inches (15 cm) long. Wrap well in plastic wrap. Store in refrigerator for up to 5 days or in freezer for several months. Cuts into twenty-four $^1/_4$ inch (6 mm) slices.

1 slice: 34 Calories; 3.8 g Total Fat; 57 mg Sodium; trace Protein; trace Carbohydrate; trace Dietary Fiber

Herbed Butter

Serve on a hot grilled beef steak or pork chops. The tarragon flavor comes through pleasantly.
Pictured on page 53.

Unsalted butter, softened (about 4 oz., 113 g)	**$1/2$ cup**	**125 mL**
Chopped fresh parsley	**2 tbsp.**	**30 mL**
Chopped fresh tarragon leaves	**1 tbsp.**	**15 mL**
Garlic clove, minced	**1**	**1**
Salt	**$1/4$ tsp.**	**1 mL**
Freshly ground pepper, sprinkle		

Whip butter with beaters in small bowl until light in color. ■ Blend in remaining 5 ingredients. Cover. Chill for 1 hour until butter can be formed into log about 6 inches (15 cm) long. Wrap well in plastic wrap. Store in refrigerator for up to 5 days or in freezer for several months. Cuts into twenty-four $1/4$ inch (6 mm) slices.

1 slice: 34 Calories; 3.8 g Total Fat; 29 mg Sodium; trace Protein; trace Carbohydrate; trace Dietary Fiber

Fresh Tartar Sauce

Serve with Salmon And Rice Patties, page 48, or other fish. Pictured on page 36.

Light mayonnaise	**$1/4$ cup**	**60 mL**
Light sour cream	**$1/4$ cup**	**60 mL**
Finely grated lemon peel	**$1/4$ tsp.**	**1 mL**
Freshly squeezed lemon juice	**2 tsp.**	**10 mL**
Chopped fresh parsley	**$1^1/2$ tsp.**	**7 mL**
Chopped fresh dill	**$1^1/2$ tsp.**	**7 mL**

Combine all 6 ingredients in small bowl. Cover. Let stand in refrigerator for 30 minutes to meld flavors. Makes $1/2$ cup (125 mL).

1 tbsp. (15 mL): 29 Calories; 2.4 g Total Fat; 61 mg Sodium; trace Protein; 2 g Carbohydrate; trace Dietary Fiber

Red Hot Sauce

Thick, red full-bodied sauce. Good as a basting or dipping sauce, or try with Steak Fajitas, page 29. Pictured on page 35.

Chopped onion	**1 cup**	**250 mL**
Garlic cloves, minced	**5**	**5**
Olive oil	**2 tsp.**	**10 mL**
Tomato sauce	**7¹/₂ oz.**	**213 mL**
Chili sauce	**¹/₃ cup**	**75 mL**
Brown sugar, packed	**¹/₃ cup**	**75 mL**
Apple cider vinegar	**¹/₄ cup**	**60 mL**
Salt	**¹/₄ tsp.**	**1 mL**
Cayenne pepper	**¹/₈-¹/₄ tsp.**	**0.5-1 mL**

Cook onion and garlic in olive oil in medium non-stick skillet for 5 minutes, stirring frequently to prevent browning, until onion is very soft. ■ Add remaining 6 ingredients. Stir well. Simmer, uncovered, for 10 minutes until sauce is reduced and thickened. Makes 1¹/₂ cups (375 mL).

2 tbsp. (30 mL): 44 Calories; 0.8 g Total Fat; 165 mg Sodium; 1 g Protein; 9 g Carbohydrate; 1 g Dietary Fiber

Note: This sauce spatters a bit and may be cooked partially covered with lid; however, it may take up to 20 minutes to reduce and thicken.

. . . .

The size, amount and shape of the food you are cooking will affect the required cooking time. Time will increase with added quantity but will decrease if the pieces are cut smaller. For example, a large 2 lb. (900 g) thick sirloin steak will take longer than if the steak was cut into individual portions, or even less time if cut into cubes and pushed onto skewers. If foods are crowded on the grill, more time will be required and rearranging the position of the food will probably be necessary. To cook a casserole or pot of beans, less time will be required if they are cooked in a shallow pan rather than a deep casserole dish.

Backyard Party

here's nothing more fun or relaxing than enjoying your backyard with family and friends. Food always seems to be a part of those times—maybe because things just taste better in the great outdoors! One of the best things about hosting a backyard party is the casual atmosphere that allows you to keep it simple. No one will expect a formal sit-down dinner, nor will they anticipate being waited on hand and foot. A supply of chilled drinks, comfortable patio furniture, and maybe a few well placed candles or outdoor lights are all you need to do to prepare your surroundings before the first guest arrives. You will need to consider a few things in advance. Plan your menu, decide how best to serve the meal, and keep in mind a few of the following tips:

▼ If you are using a gas barbecue, check that the propane tank is full, or that you have a spare one full and ready to switch if necessary. If you are grilling more than one type of food, or if you want to keep food warm before you serve it, consider borrowing a second barbecue from one of your neighbors.

▼ To be safe, set the barbecue away from where guests will be mingling, and away from the side of the house. Because of the quantity of food that will be on the grill, have a spray bottle filled with water on hand to handle very small flare-ups, and baking soda to tackle larger grease flames. See Grilling Safety Tips, pages 8 and 9.

▼ Keep drinks buried in coolers filled with ice. Place strategically around the yard. Use plastic glasses and provide a recycling container for empty cans and bottles.

▼ The best way to serve food for this kind of get-together is buffet style, but remember that hot weather can turn cold dishes bad in minutes. Wait until everyone is ready to eat before setting out food. Or you may wish to set up the buffet table inside the house.

▼ Consider using disposable plates and cutlery, keeping in mind that hard-to-cut foods such as steak are difficult to manage with flimsy cutlery or plates. If guests are balancing plates on their lap, you may want to serve just fork food.

▼ Borrow or rent chairs and tables so that everyone can be seated comfortably. Consider placing tables and chairs around the yard to keep guests from congregating in one spot.

▼ As evening approaches, the temperature might drop to an uncomfortable level. Candles, patio lamps and, where local laws permit, wood fires in an enclosed pit, can all help to extend the party well into the evening. But you may want to be prepared for the option of moving everyone indoors in case the weather deteriorates too much.

▼ For a large crowd, keep the menu simple. Quick cooking foods such as hamburgers, hot dogs or sausages, boneless chicken breasts, etc. can be grilled and served with a minimum of delay and fuss. Prepare a selection of cold dishes in advance and serve when everyone is ready to eat.

▼ Create a timetable for cooking, beginning with the item that will take the longest to cook. Keep in mind that there may be recipes that require different temperature settings on the barbecue, or some where indoor cooking will ensure that everything is ready at the same time.

▼ To save time or to ensure that meat is thoroughly cooked, partially cook vegetables, chicken (bone in), ribs, roasts or other thick cuts of meat indoors, before barbecuing.

Patio Sticky Ribs

Glossy and dark. Sticky and delicious.

	18 3-rib sections	36 3-rib sections	54 3-rib sections
Pork side ribs Water, to cover	3¼ lbs. (1.5 kg)	6.5 lbs. (3 kg)	9 lbs. (4 kg)
Ketchup	⅓ cup (75 mL)	⅔ cup (150 mL)	1 cup (250 mL)
Liquid honey	2 tbsp. (30 mL)	¼ cup (60 mL)	⅓ cup (75 mL)
Frozen concentrated orange juice, thawed	1 tbsp. (15 mL)	2 tbsp. (30 mL)	3 tbsp. (50 mL)
Water	1 tbsp. (15 mL)	2 tbsp. (30 mL)	3 tbsp. (50 mL)
Soy sauce	1 tbsp. (15 mL)	2 tbsp. (30 mL)	3 tbsp. (50 mL)
White wine vinegar	1 tbsp. (15 mL)	2 tbsp. (30 mL)	3 tbsp. (50 mL)
Worcestershire sauce	1 tbsp. (15 mL)	2 tbsp. (30 mL)	3 tbsp. (50 mL)

Boil ribs in water, covered, in large Dutch oven for 45 to 60 minutes until almost tender. Drain. Cool. Pat dry. ■ Combine remaining 7 ingredients in small bowl. Dab sauce over both sides of ribs. Marinate in refrigerator for 1 hour to let sauce set. Preheat barbecue to low. Cook ribs on greased grill for about 5 minutes per side, dabbing on more sauce until ribs are glazed and sticky. Reheat sauce to boiling to serve. Serves 8, 14 or 20.

1 serving: 257 Calories; 16.7 g Total Fat; 357 mg Sodium; 17 g Protein; 9 g Carbohydrate; trace Dietary Fiber

Chops For A Crowd

Rich brown appearance with a mild tasting sauce.

	20 pork chops (3 cups, 750 mL, sauce)	40 pork chops (6 cups, 1.5 L, sauce)	60 pork chops (9 cups, 2.3 L, sauce)
Chopped onion	$^3/_4$ cup (175 mL)	$1^1/_2$ cups (375 mL)	$2^1/_4$ cups (560 mL)
Garlic clove(s), minced	1	2	3
Canola oil	2 tsp. (10 mL)	4 tsp. (20 mL)	2 tbsp. (30 mL)
Tomato sauce	$7^1/_2$ oz. (213 mL) can	14 oz. (398 mL) can	21.5 oz. (632 mL) (1 small + 1 large can)
Chili sauce	$^1/_2$ cup (125 mL)	1 cup (250 mL)	$1^1/_2$ cups (375 mL)
Ketchup	$^1/_2$ cup (125 mL)	1 cup (250 mL)	$1^1/_2$ cups (375 mL)
Beer	$^1/_2$ cup (125 mL)	1 cup (250 mL)	$1^1/_2$ cups (375 mL)
Apple cider vinegar	$^1/_4$ cup (60 mL)	$^1/_2$ cup (125 mL)	$^3/_4$ cup (175 mL)
Cooking molasses	$^1/_4$ cup (60 mL)	$^1/_2$ cup (125 mL)	$^3/_4$ cup (175 mL)
Brown sugar, packed	$^1/_4$ cup (60 mL)	$^1/_2$ cup (125 mL)	$^3/_4$ cup (175 mL)
Dry mustard	$1^1/_2$ tsp. (7 mL)	1 tbsp. (15 mL)	$4^1/_2$ tsp. (22 mL)
Worcestershire sauce	1 tsp. (5 mL)	2 tsp. (10 mL)	1 tbsp. (15 mL)
Hot pepper sauce	$^1/_4$ tsp. (1 mL)	$^1/_2$ tsp. (2 mL)	$^3/_4$ tsp. (4 mL)
Liquid smoke	$^1/_8$ tsp. (0.5 mL)	$^1/_4$ tsp. (1 mL)	$^1/_2$ tsp. (2 mL)
Pork loin chops	7.5 lbs. (3.4 kg)	15 lbs. (6.8 kg)	23 lbs. (10.4 kg)
Seasoned salt	$1^1/_2$ tsp. (7 mL)	1 tbsp. (15 mL)	$4^1/_2$ tsp. (22 mL)
Freshly ground pepper	$1^1/_2$ tsp. (7 mL)	1 tbsp. (15 mL)	$4^1/_2$ tsp. (22 mL)

Preheat barbecue to medium. Sauté onion and garlic in oil in large saucepan, stirring frequently, until onion is soft. ■ Stir in next 11 ingredients. Bring mixture to a boil. Reduce heat and simmer, uncovered, for 20 minutes. ■ Season pork chops with seasoned salt and pepper. Place on greased grill. Close lid. Cook for 15 to 20 minutes until desired doneness. Heat sauce. Dip each chop, using tongs, into sauce. Place chops in large greased casserole or roaster. Pour any remaining sauce over. Cover. Keep warm in low oven or barbecue until ready to serve. Serves 12, 24 or 48.

1 serving: 463 Calories; 27 g Total Fat; 676 mg Sodium; 34 g Protein; 19 g Carbohydrate; 1 g Dietary Fiber

Teriyaki Chicken For A Party

These only take a few minutes to put together. Everyone enjoys these. They brown nicely without burning.

	16 pieces	32 pieces	48 pieces
Low-sodium soy sauce	$^3/_4$ cup (175 mL)	$1^1/_2$ cups (375 mL)	$2^1/_3$ cups (575 mL)
Brown sugar, packed	$^1/_3$ cup (75 mL)	$^2/_3$ cup (150 mL)	1 cup (250 mL)
Ground ginger	2 tsp. (10 mL)	4 tsp. (20 mL)	2 tbsp. (30 mL)
Garlic cloves, minced	2	4	6
Boneless, skinless chicken breast halves (or thighs)	4 lbs. (1.8 kg)	$7^1/_2$ lbs. (3.4 kg)	12.5 lbs. (5.7 kg)

Stir soy sauce, brown sugar, ginger and garlic together in medium bowl until brown sugar is dissolved. ■ Dip each chicken piece into marinade to coat thoroughly. Stack chicken pieces in deep casserole or roaster. Cover. Marinate in refrigerator until ready to barbecue. Preheat barbecue to medium. Drain and discard marinade. Place chicken on greased grill. Close lid. Cook for 10 to 15 minutes per side until no longer pink. Serves 16, 32 or 48.

1 serving: 148 Calories; 1.4 g Total Fat; 516 mg Sodium; 27 g Protein; 5 g Carbohydrate; trace Dietary Fiber

Beef

grilling is a wonderful way to achieve the utmost flavor from steaks or roasts. The trimmed lean beef we buy today, when enjoyed in the proper portions, is so healthy for us. Use a marinade to infuse flavors or to tenderize less than prime cuts. Pick a more traditional Teriyaki Sirloin or have fun with Steak Fajitas. For a really quick impressive lunch, serve Sake Beef Rolls.

Japanese Grilled Beef

An excellent quick meal for two. Serve with steamed rice and Japanese Ginger Sauce, page 20, for dipping.

Garlic cloves	2	2
Rice vinegar	$^1/_4$ cup	60 mL
Granulated sugar	1 tbsp.	15 mL
Toasted sesame seeds	2 tbsp.	30 mL
Green onion (about 4 inches, 10 cm, in length)	1	1
Sesame oil	2 tsp.	10 mL
Low-sodium soy sauce	$^1/_4$ cup	60 mL
Zucchini, sliced on the diagonal into $^1/_2$ inch (12 mm) slices	1	1
Portabello mushroom slices	6	6
Thinly sliced top sirloin ($^1/_4$ inch, 6 mm, thick)	$^1/_2$ lb.	225 g

Process first 7 ingredients in blender until smooth. Makes about $^2/_3$ cup (150 mL) marinade. ■ Place zucchini, mushrooms and steak in sealable plastic bag. Pour rice vinegar mixture into bag. Marinate in refrigerator overnight, turning once or twice to distribute marinade. Drain and discard marinade. Preheat lightly sprayed electric grill to high. Cook vegetable pieces on grill for about 2 minutes per side until tender-crisp. Remove to serving plate. Cook steak pieces on grill for about 45 seconds per side until just seared but not overcooked. Serves 2.

1 serving: 280 Calories; 12.7 g Total Fat; 1234 mg Sodium; 24 g Protein; 19 g Carbohydrate; 4 g Dietary Fiber

Steak Fajitas

Serve with Red Hot Sauce, page 23, sour cream, shredded lettuce and grated sharp Cheddar cheese. Pictured on page 35.

Beer	¹/₂ **cup**	**125 mL**
Lime juice	¹/₄ **cup**	**60 mL**
Water	¹/₄ **cup**	**60 mL**
Garlic cloves, minced	**2**	**2**
Cajun seasoning	**1 - 2 tsp.**	**5-10 mL**
Freshly ground pepper, sprinkle		
Flank steak (scored on 1 side)	**1¹/₄ lbs.**	**560 g**
Canola oil	**1 tbsp.**	**15 mL**
Large onions, cut into ¹/₂ inch (12 mm) slices	**2**	**2**
Red pepper, quartered and seeded	**1**	**1**
Orange or yellow pepper, quartered and seeded	**1**	**1**
Flour tortillas (10 inch, 25 cm, size)	**8**	**8**

Combine first 6 ingredients in small bowl. Makes 1 cup (250 mL) marinade. ■ Place steak in sealable plastic bag or shallow casserole. Pour marinade over steak. Seal bag. Marinate in refrigerator for 6 hours or overnight. Preheat lightly sprayed electric grill to high. Drain and reserve marinade. Sear steak for 1 minute per side. Baste with marinade. Cook on high for 10 minutes per side, basting occasionally. ■ Combine remaining marinade (about ¹/₂ cup, 125 mL) with oil. ■ Cook onion and both peppers on hot grill, turning and basting with oil mixture several times, until tender-crisp. Discard any remaining marinade. Remove vegetables to cutting board. Sliver peppers, cut onion slices into quarters and cut steak into thin slices on diagonal. ■ Sprinkle some water with fingers, on each tortilla. Stack and enclose in foil. Heat for about 3 minutes per side until warm. Divide steak and vegetables among warmed tortillas. Roll up. Makes 8 fajitas.

1 fajita: 313 Calories; 7.6 g Total Fat; 243 mg Sodium; 22 g Protein; 37 g Carbohydrate; 1 g Dietary Fiber

....

Use the "touch test" to determine doneness of meat and poultry rather than cutting with a knife. Press the center of the meat with your index finger (or with tongs). Rare will feel soft and the juices will run red, medium-rare will feel springy with some resistance and pink juices, and well done will feel firm and unyielding with broth-colored juice (or clear, if poultry).

Herbed Steak Slices

The herbs share their flavor with the steak. Easy to make and so impressive to serve. Pictured on page 53.

Flank steak	**1¹/₂ lbs.**	**680 g**
Canola oil	**2 tbsp.**	**30 mL**
Balsamic vinegar	**1 tbsp.**	**15 mL**
Garlic cloves, minced	**4**	**4**
Chopped fresh parsley	**¹/₄ cup**	**60 mL**
Chopped fresh thyme leaves	**1 tbsp.**	**15 mL**
Chopped fresh rosemary leaves	**¹/₂-1 tbsp.**	**7-15 mL**
Salt	**1 tsp.**	**5 mL**
Freshly ground pepper	**1 tsp.**	**5 mL**

Pound steak to even thickness with meat mallet. ■ Combine remaining 8 ingredients in mini food chopper or pound together with mortar and pestle until paste-like. Spread over steak. Roll steak, jelly-roll style, lengthwise. Tie with butcher's string to secure. Preheat barbecue to medium. Place roll on greased grill over drip pan using indirect heat cooking method (see page 7). Cook for 1 to 1¹/₂ hours, turning 3 times, until desired doneness. Let stand tented in foil for 10 to 15 minutes. Cut into ³/₄ inch (2 cm) diagonal slices. Serves 6.

1 serving: 237 Calories; 13.5 g Total Fat; 509 mg Sodium; 26 g Protein; 1 g Carbohydrate; trace Dietary Fiber

So' West Steak

Increase the chilies in the flavorful paste for more kick. Scoring the steak helps the flavors penetrate.

Dried crushed chilies	**¹/₂-1 tsp.**	**2-5 mL**
Garlic cloves, crushed	**2**	**2**
Brown sugar, packed	**1 tbsp.**	**15 mL**
Freshly ground pepper, generous sprinkle		
Dried thyme, crushed	**¹/₂-1 tsp.**	**2-5 mL**
Canola oil	**2 tsp.**	**10 mL**
Paprika	**1 tsp.**	**5 mL**
Flank steak	**1¹/₂ lbs.**	**680 g**
Salt, to taste (optional)		

(continued on next page)

Combine first 7 ingredients in small dish to make paste. ■ Score steak on both sides in diamond pattern. Spread seasoning on both sides of steak. Place on plate. Cover. Let stand in refrigerator for 1 hour. Preheat lightly sprayed electric grill to high. Cook steak on grill for 6 minutes per side. ■ Sprinkle with salt. Remove to cutting board. Let stand for 5 minutes before slicing on sharp diagonal across grain into thin slices. Serves 6.

1 serving: 216 Calories; 10.4 g Total Fat; 58 mg Sodium; 26 g Protein; 3 g Carbohydrate; trace Dietary Fiber

Spicy Eye Of Round Roast

Marinate this a long time for the most flavor. The bacon plus grilling combine to make this much better than any oven roasted beef!

Canned tomato juice	**10 oz.**	**284 mL**
Lemon juice	**$1/_4$ cup**	**60 mL**
Worcestershire sauce	**1 tbsp.**	**15 mL**
Garlic powder	**$1/_2$ tsp.**	**2 mL**
Onion powder	**$1/_2$ tsp.**	**2 mL**
Ground allspice	**$1/_2$ tsp.**	**2 mL**
Chili powder	**$1/_2$ tsp.**	**2 mL**
Seasoned salt	**1 tsp.**	**5 mL**
Eye of round beef roast	**$2^1/_2$-3 lbs.**	**1.1-1.4 kg**
Bacon slices	**4**	**4**

Combine first 8 ingredients in blender or small bowl. Makes $1^1/_2$ cups (375 mL) marinade. ■ Place roast in large sealable plastic bag. Pour marinade over roast. Seal bag. Set bag in large bowl. Marinate in refrigerator for up to 48 hours, turning occasionally. Drain and discard marinade. ■ Secure bacon slices over top of roast with wooden picks. Preheat barbecue to high. Place roast on grill over drip pan using indirect heat cooking method, for about 40 minutes until roast and bacon are well browned. Reduce heat to medium. Close lid. Cook for 40 to 50 minutes until roast tests medium or medium rare. Roast may be tough if overcooked. Let stand for 10 minutes before slicing very thinly. Serves 8.

1 serving: 212 Calories; 8.9 g Total Fat; 210 mg Sodium; 30 g Protein; 1 g Carbohydrate; trace Dietary Fiber

Steak 'N' Veggies

It's best to do this on a large barbecue surface starting with potatoes and squash. Do the steak once the vegetables are almost done and you'll have your complete meal ready at the same time.

Garlic cloves, minced	**2-3**	**2-3**
Olive oil	**¹/₄ cup**	**60 mL**
Parsley flakes	**1 tsp.**	**5 mL**
Paprika	**1 tsp.**	**5 mL**
Cayenne pepper	**¹/₁₆ tsp.**	**0.5 mL**
Freshly ground pepper, sprinkle		
Medium potatoes, with peel, cut into ¹/₂ inch (12 mm) thick slices	**3**	**3**
Winter squash, shell on, cut into quarters and then cut in half crosswise	**1**	**1**
Top sirloin steak (cut ³/₄ inch, 2 cm, thick and trimmed of fat)	**1 lb.**	**454 g**

Combine first 6 ingredients in small bowl. ■ Brush potato slices with some oil mixture. Preheat lightly sprayed electric grill to high. Cook potato slices for about 30 minutes, turning frequently, until tender and browned. ■ Repeat with squash but only brush inside flesh with olive oil mixture. Cook, shell side down, for about 5 minutes. Turn over. Cook for 15 to 20 minutes until squash is tender. ■ Cook steak on hot grill for 7 to 8 minutes per side, brushing with remaining oil mixture and turning once, until preferred doneness. Cut into ¹/₄ inch (6 mm) diagonal slices to serve. Serves 4.

1 serving: 389 Calories; 19 g Total Fat; 62 mg Sodium; 27 g Protein; 29 g Carbohydrate; 4 g Dietary Fiber

Stuffed Steak

The "stuffing" shows so attractively once the steak is cut. Wonderful basil and tomato flavor. Pictured on page 108.

Basil pesto	**¹/₃ cup**	**75 mL**
Sun-dried tomato pieces, soaked in boiling water for 10 minutes and then chopped	**6**	**6**
Freshly ground pepper, generous sprinkle		
Top sirloin steak (1¹/₂ inches, 3.8 cm, thick), trimmed of fat	**2 lbs.**	**900 g**

(continued on next page)

Preheat barbecue to medium. Combine pesto, tomato, and pepper in small bowl.
■ Cut 3 or 4 straight gashes lengthwise down 1 side of steak, about $^1/_2$ inch (12 mm) deep. Spread pesto mixture inside gashes. Carefully place on ungreased grill over indirect heat. Close lid. Cook for about 35 minutes until desired doneness. Slice on sharp diagonal across grain. Serves 8.

1 serving: 170 Calories; 7.5 g Total Fat; 53 mg Sodium; 23 g Protein; 2 g Carbohydrate; 1 g Dietary Fiber

Teriyaki Sirloin

It's best to cook this steak outdoors on the barbecue but a saucepan lid can be used as a cover on an electric indoor grill if you prefer.

Dark soy sauce	**$^2/_3$ cup**	**150 mL**
Lemon juice	**2 tbsp.**	**30 mL**
Red wine vinegar	**2 tbsp.**	**30 mL**
Garlic cloves, minced	**2**	**2**
Ground ginger	**2 tsp.**	**10 mL**
Brown sugar, packed	**2 tbsp.**	**30 mL**
Ketchup	**1 tbsp.**	**15 mL**
Top sirloin steak ($^3/_4$ inch, 2 cm, thick), trimmed of fat	**1 lb.**	**454 g**

Combine first 7 ingredients in small bowl. Makes 1 cup (250 mL) marinade. ■ Place steak in sealable plastic bag or shallow casserole. Pour marinade over steak. Seal bag. Marinate in refrigerator overnight. Drain and discard marinade. Preheat barbecue to high. Sear steak on greased grill for about 30 seconds per side. Close lid. Cook for 3 to 5 minutes per side until desired doneness. Serves 4.

1 serving: 133 Calories; 4.2 g Total Fat; 1512 mg Sodium; 25 g Protein; 7 g Carbohydrate; trace Dietary Fiber

Sake Beef Rolls

The pleasant heat from the wasabi and pickled peppers mingles with Japanese sake for an unusual but delicious entrée.

Cornstarch	1 tsp.	5 mL
Thin large deli roast beef slices	4	4
Green onions, cut into 3 inch (7.5 cm) pieces	2	2
and then cut lengthwise into slivers		
Julienned zucchini slivers (3 inch, 7.5 cm, pieces)	¹/₄ cup	60 mL
Thinly sliced fresh brown mushrooms	¹/₄ cup	60 mL
Freshly ground pepper, sprinkle		
Hot pickled peppers, drained and chopped	1 tbsp.	15 mL
Sake (rice wine)	¹/₄ cup	60 mL
Dry (or alcohol-free) sherry	2 tbsp.	30 mL
Low-sodium soy sauce	2 tbsp.	30 mL
Brown sugar, packed	2 tbsp.	30 mL
Lemon juice	1 tbsp.	15 mL
Wasabi paste	¹/₂ tsp.	2 mL

Sprinkle cornstarch evenly over beef slices. ■ Divide green onion, zucchini and mushrooms along bottom edge of each beef slice. Sprinkle with pepper. ■ Divide pickled peppers evenly over vegetables. Fold bottom edge of meat up and over vegetables. Roll up all the way. Tie with butcher's string near both ends. ■ Combine remaining 6 ingredients in glass pie plate or shallow casserole. Makes ¹/₂ cup (125 mL) marinade. Coat rolls in marinade. Cover. Marinate in refrigerator for 2 hours. Preheat lightly sprayed electric grill to medium-high. Drain and discard marinade. Cook rolls on grill for about 8 minutes, turning a quarter turn several times, until desired doneness. Cut into diagonal slices to serve. Makes 4 rolls.

1 roll: 213 Calories; 5.3 g Total Fat; 334 mg Sodium; 30 g Protein; 8 g Carbohydrate; trace Dietary Fiber

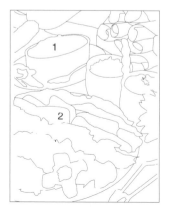

1. Red Hot Sauce, page 23
2. Steak Fajitas, page 29

Steak With Mushrooms And Onions

Enhancing the flavor of commercial Italian dressing makes the marinade quick to prepare.

Italian dressing	**¹/₂ cup**	**125 mL**
Red wine vinegar	**2 tbsp.**	**30 mL**
Garlic clove, minced	**1**	**1**
Freshly ground pepper, sprinkle		
Whole portabello mushrooms	**2**	**2**
Large red (or Spanish) onion, cut into	**1**	**1**
** thick whole slices**		
Top sirloin steak, trimmed of fat	**1 lb.**	**454 g**
Seasoned salt	**¹/₂ tsp.**	**2 mL**
Freshly ground pepper, sprinkle		

Combine dressing, red wine vinegar, garlic and pepper in glass pie plate. Makes ²/₃ cup (150 mL) marinade. ■ Remove stems from mushrooms and reserve for another purpose. Scrape and discard black "gills" from around underside of mushrooms with a spoon. Place mushrooms in marinade. Turn to coat. Marinate in refrigerator for 30 minutes. ■ Preheat lightly sprayed electric grill to high. Drain and boil marinade for 5 minutes. Reserve for basting. Cook mushrooms and red onion on grill for 7 to 8 minutes, turning and basting with reserved marinade several times, until onions are tender-crisp. ■ Sear steak on grill for 1 minute per side. Sprinkle both sides with salt and pepper. Brush with marinade. Cook for 3 to 4 minutes per side until desired doneness. Discard any remaining marinade. Remove to cutting board. Cut into thin slices across grain. Arrange on platter. Cut mushrooms into thin slices. Quarter onion slices. Arrange over top of steak to serve. Serves 4.

1 serving: 325 Calories; 23.9 g Total Fat; 651 mg Sodium; 20 g Protein; 9 g Carbohydrate; 2 g Dietary Fiber

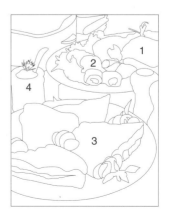

1. Rice And Salmon Patties, page 48
2. Rolled Sole With Sesame, page 132
3. Grilled Pepper And Tomato Sandwiches, page 134
4. Fresh Tartar Sauce, page 22

Burgers & Sandwiches

e've made traditional fare more exciting and nutritious in this section. There's a lot of variety and goodness in patties when lentils and vegetables are added. Try Zucchini Burgers, Crunchy Thai Wraps or Steak Donair for your next after-the-game crowd. Who says sandwiches are boring!

Zucchini Burgers

Dress up these moist burgers with lettuce, tomatoes and other condiments.

Extra lean ground beef	**12 oz.**	**340 g**
Grated zucchini, with peel	**2 cups**	**500 mL**
Finely ground soda cracker crumbs	**1 cup**	**250 mL**
Garlic cloves, minced	**2**	**2**
Onion salt	**1 tsp.**	**5 mL**
Egg white (large), fork-beaten	**1**	**1**
Sun-dried tomato pesto	**4 tsp.**	**20 mL**
Hamburger buns, split	**4**	**4**
Lettuce leaves	**4**	**4**
Large tomato slices	**4**	**4**

Combine first 7 ingredients in medium bowl. Divide into 4 portions. Form into evenly flattened 4 to 5 inch (10 to 12.5 cm) patties. Preheat lightly sprayed electric grill to medium-high. Cook patties for 6 to 8 minutes per side until beef is no longer pink.
■ Toast buns, cut side down, on grill. Place patties in buns. Add lettuce and tomato. Makes 4 burgers.

1 burger: 394 Calories; 14.2 g Total Fat; 864 mg Sodium; 23 g Protein; 43 g Carbohydrate; 3 g Dietary Fiber

Variation: Substitute same amount of basil pesto for sun-dried tomato pesto.

Oriental Burgers

Darken nicely with noticeable "grill" lines. Mild flavor of garlic and teriyaki. The bean sprouts and red onion are a must to complete this burger.

Lean ground beef	**1 lb.**	**454 g**
Fine dry bread crumbs	**¹/₄ cup**	**60 mL**
Canned water chestnuts, drained and chopped	**8 oz.**	**227 mL**
Chopped fresh parsley, packed	**¹/₄ cup**	**60 mL**
Egg white (large)	**1**	**1**
Onion salt	**1 tsp.**	**5 mL**
Garlic clove, minced	**1**	**1**
Sesame seeds, toasted	**2 tsp.**	**10 mL**
Freshly ground pepper, generous sprinkle		
Teriyaki Basting Sauce, page 81 (or commercial)	**¹/₃ cup**	**75 mL**
Hamburger buns, split	**6**	**6**
Very thinly sliced large red onion rings	**6**	**6**
Fresh bean sprouts	**2 cups**	**500 mL**

Combine first 9 ingredients in medium bowl. Mix well. Form into 6 flattened patties, 4 inches (10 cm) in diameter. Preheat lightly sprayed electric grill to medium-high. Cook patties on grill for 6 to 8 minutes per side until beef is no longer pink. ■ Brush patties with 2 tbsp. (30 mL) teriyaki sauce. Remove patties to plate. Cover with foil. ■ Toast buns, cut side down, on hot grill. ■ Brush red onion rings with 2 tsp. (10 mL) oil. Preheat grill to high. Cook each side of onion rings for 2 to 3 minutes until slightly soft. ■ Sauté bean sprouts on flat part of grill in remaining teriyaki sauce and oil until tender-crisp. (Or use skillet and stir-fry for 1 to 2 minutes.) Insert red onion, bean sprouts and patty into each bun. Makes 6 burgers.

1 burger: 338 Calories; 9.6 g Total Fat; 827 mg Sodium; 21 g Protein; 41 g Carbohydrate; 2 g Dietary Fiber

. . . .

Cooking times for meats and vegetables may have to be adjusted when cooking outdoors if there is a wind, or if temperatures are on the cool side. Food will take longer to cook in winter than in summer. Additional time will also be required if the meat has just been taken from the refrigerator, or if it is not fully defrosted.

Bratwurst Buns

Condiments could include sauerkraut, hot pickled peppers, chopped onion and grainy mustard.

Bratwurst sausages (about ³/₄ lb., 340 g)	6	6
Water	1 cup	250 mL
Beer	12 oz.	355 mL
Bay leaves	2	2
Caraway seeds	2 tsp.	10 mL
Grainy mustard	3 tbsp.	50 mL
Liquid honey	3 tbsp.	50 mL
Oblong-shaped crusty buns	6	6

Poke sausage in 3 places with fork. ■ Bring water, beer, bay leaves, caraway seeds and sausages to a boil in large saucepan for 5 minutes. Drain and discard liquid, including bay leaves. Cut 2 or 3 diagonal slashes on 1 side of sausages. ■ Combine mustard and honey in small cup. Preheat barbecue to medium. Cook sausages on greased grill for about 5 minutes, turning and basting with mustard sauce, until glazed and golden. ■ Serve sausages in crusty buns. Makes 6 sausage buns.

1 sausage bun: 366 Calories; 16.8 g Total Fat; 733 mg Sodium; 13 g Protein; 40 g Carbohydrate; 1 g Dietary Fiber

Garlic Toast And Steak Sandwiches

Generous stack of grilled steak on a golden toasted crispy bun. No "tug-of-war" with these tender strips.

Top sirloin steak (2 inches, 5 cm, thick), trimmed of fat	1¹/₂ lbs.	680 g
Seasoned salt, sprinkle		
Garlic powder, light sprinkle		
Freshly ground pepper, sprinkle		
Tub margarine	¹/₄ cup	60 mL
Parsley flakes	1 tsp.	5 mL
Garlic clove, minced	1	1
Large round Kaiser (or other) buns, split	6	6
Finely chopped red onion	¹/₃ cup	75 mL

(continued on next page)

Season steak on both sides with seasoned salt, garlic powder and pepper. Preheat lightly sprayed electric grill to high. Sear steak on grill for 2 minutes per side. Reduce heat to low. Cook steak for 2 to 3 minutes until desired doneness. ■ Combine margarine, parsley and garlic in small bowl. ■ Spread over cut side of bun halves. Place buns, buttered side down, on grill to toast. Thinly slice steak on diagonal across grain. Divide steak slices evenly on bottom half of each bun. ■ Divide red onion evenly over steak. Cover with top half of bun. Eat while warm. Makes 6 sandwiches.

1 sandwich: 358 Calories; 13 g Total Fat; 459 mg Sodium; 28 g Protein; 31 g Carbohydrate; 1 g Dietary Fiber

Special Grilled Cheese

A true "grilled" cheese—with the lines to prove it! Using old, sharp Cheddar is the key to the flavor.

Thin sharp Cheddar cheese slices (about 8 oz., 225 g)	8	8
Diagonal French bread slices, cut about 1/2 inch (12 mm) thick	8	8
Large tomato slices, cut 1/4 inch (6 mm) thick	4	4
Freshly ground pepper, sprinkle		
Tub margarine	2¹/₂ tbsp.	37 mL
Garlic clove, minced	1	1

Preheat lightly sprayed electric grill to medium. Lay 1 cheese slice on 1 bread slice. Lay 1 tomato slice over cheese. Sprinkle with pepper. Cover with 1 cheese slice. Place 1 bread slice over top. Repeat to make 4 sandwiches. ■ Combine margarine and garlic in small bowl. Spread 1/2 of mixture over top sides of sandwiches. Turn sandwiches over. Place, buttered side down, on grill. Spread remaining margarine mixture over top sides of sandwiches. Cook until toasted and cheese is melted. Makes 4 sandwiches.

1 sandwich: 440 Calories; 27.3 g Total Fat; 736 mg Sodium; 19 g Protein; 30 g Carbohydrate; 1 g Dietary Fiber

Polynesian Burgers

Garnish these juicy burgers with lettuce, tomatoes or other condiments of your choice.

Lean ground pork	12 oz.	340 g
Lean ground beef	4 oz.	113 g
Fine dry bread crumbs	$^1/_3$ cup	75 mL
Low-sodium soy sauce	3 tbsp.	50 mL
Garlic clove, minced	1	1
Onion powder	$^1/_4$ tsp.	1 mL
Freshly ground pepper, sprinkle		
Finely chopped green pepper	$^1/_4$ cup	60 mL
Canned pineapple slices, drained and juice reserved	4	4
Reserved pineapple juice		
Whole wheat hamburger buns, split	4	4
Hot pepper jelly	3 tbsp.	50 mL

Preheat lightly sprayed electric grill to medium-high. Combine first 7 ingredients in medium bowl. Divide into 8 equal portions. Flatten each portion into 4 inch (10 cm) patty. ■ Sprinkle 1 tbsp. (15 mL) green pepper over each of 4 patties. Lay pineapple slice over green pepper. Cover with remaining patties. Seal edges well to enclose green pepper and pineapple slices. ■ Cook patties on grill for 4 to 5 minutes per side, basting with reserved pineapple juice several times, until beef is no longer pink. ■ Grill buns, cut side down, for about 2 minutes until lightly toasted. Spread about $^1/_2$ to 1 tsp. (2 to 5 mL) jelly on each bun half. Fill with patty. Makes 4 burgers.

1 burger: 344 Calories; 8.3 g Total Fat; 780 mg Sodium; 22 g Protein; 46 g Carbohydrate; 3 g Dietary Fiber

* * *

tip

Keep burger condiments—lettuce, tomato slice, ketchup, mustard, pickles, mayonnaise, etc.—in the refrigerator until just before serving regardless of whether indoors or outdoors. The crispness and chill will contrast nicely with the hot burger in that first bite. If it's a buffet, the condiments will be sitting at room temperature for an extended period of time so all the more reason to set them out chilled.

Chicken Caesar Burgers

Wow! What a great summer meal. Easy to prepare; quick to cook.

Light salad dressing (or mayonnaise)	**$^1/_4$ cup**	**60 mL**
Light sour cream	**$^1/_4$ cup**	**60 mL**
Olive oil	**1 tbsp.**	**15 mL**
Garlic cloves, minced	**2**	**2**
Lemon juice	**2 tsp.**	**10 mL**
Red wine vinegar	**2 tsp.**	**10 mL**
Worcestershire sauce	**2 tsp.**	**10 mL**
Granulated sugar	**2 tsp.**	**10 mL**
Anchovy paste (optional)	**$1^1/_2$ tsp.**	**7 mL**
Dry mustard	**$^1/_2$ tsp.**	**2 mL**
Boneless, skinless chicken breast halves (about 1 lb., 454 g)	**4**	**4**
Large red onion rings	**4**	**4**
Large hamburger (or Kaiser) buns	**4**	**4**
Torn romaine lettuce	**2 cups**	**500 mL**
Grated Parmesan cheese	**1 tbsp.**	**15 mL**

Combine first 10 ingredients in small bowl. Makes $^2/_3$ cup (150 mL) sauce. Pour $^1/_2$ of sauce into shallow glass casserole. Cover and reserve remaining sauce in refrigerator. ■ Pound chicken breast halves with mallet to even thickness. Place in casserole in single layer. Coat with sauce. Cover. Let stand in refrigerator for 2 hours or overnight. Preheat lightly sprayed electric grill to high. Remove chicken from sauce. Discard excess sauce in casserole. Cook chicken on grill for about 20 minutes, turning several times until no longer pink inside. ■ Grill red onion rings for 4 to 5 minutes per side. Toast buns on both sides on hot grill. Combine lettuce with reserved sauce and Parmesan cheese in medium bowl. Pile lettuce mixture on bottom half of bun. Top with grilled red onion ring, chicken breast half and second half of bun. Repeat. Makes 4 burgers.

1 burger: 428 Calories; 16.7 g Total Fat; 634 mg Sodium; 36 g Protein; 31 g Carbohydrate; 2 g Dietary Fiber

Variation: Substitute $^2/_3$ cup (150 mL) commercial Caesar dressing for first 10 ingredients—$^1/_3$ cup (75 mL) to marinate chicken and $^1/_3$ cup (75 mL) to toss with lettuce.

German Sandwiches

What a yummy sandwich! Sauerkraut gives a nip, not a bite—keeps the flavor smooth. Caraway flavor is subtle.

Lean ground pork	1 lb.	454 g
Garlic clove, minced	1	1
Drained and finely chopped dill pickles	1/4 cup	60 mL
Sauerkraut, drained and chopped	3/4 cup	175 mL
Large egg, fork-beaten	1	1
Prepared mustard	1 tbsp.	15 mL
Seasoned salt	1 tsp.	5 mL
Caraway seeds, crushed with a mortar and pestle (optional)	1/4 tsp.	1 mL
Fresh whole wheat bread crumbs (about 2 slices, processed)	1 cup	250 mL
Swiss cheese slices (about 6 oz., 170 g)	6	6
Rye bread slices (about 3/4 inch, 2 cm, thick)	12	12
Tub margarine	1/4 cup	60 mL
Dijon mustard	2 tbsp.	30 mL
Tomato slices	6	6
Lettuce leaves	6	6

Preheat barbecue to medium-high. Combine first 9 ingredients in large bowl. Divide into 6 equal balls. Form into flattened patties about $3^{1}/_{2}$ x $5^{1}/_{2}$ inches (9 x 14 cm) to fit size of bread. Place patties on greased grill. Close lid. Cook for 6 to 7 minutes per side. Turn. Cook for 3 to 4 minutes until no pink remains. ■ Lay cheese slice over each patty. Remove to plate. Tent with foil or cover. ■ Spread rye bread slices with margarine on 1 side. Cook, buttered side down, for about 2 minutes until golden. Turn over. Cook until golden. Remove from grill. ■ Top 1 bread slice, on buttered side, with mustard, tomato slice, patty, and lettuce. Cover with second slice of bread, buttered side down. Repeat with remaining bread, patties and condiments. Cut in half to serve. Makes 6 sandwiches.

1 sandwich: 432 Calories; 21.9 g Total Fat; 1028 mg Sodium; 25 g Protein; 35 g Carbohydrate; 3 g Dietary Fiber

· ·

For a great weekday timesaver, grill extra patties and other meats on the weekend. Either keep in the refrigerator if being used on Monday or Tuesday, or freeze for later use.

Luau Sandwiches

Marinade permeates the chicken slightly. Juicy sweetness from pineapple juice but with a nip from the hot pepper jelly.

Low-sodium soy sauce	$^1/_4$ cup	60 mL
Reserved pineapple juice	2 tbsp.	30 mL
Garlic clove, minced	1	1
Ground ginger	$^1/_2$ tsp.	2 mL
Brown sugar, packed	$1^1/_2$ tsp.	7 mL
Boneless, skinless chicken breast halves, (about 1 lb., 454 g), pounded to even thickness	4	4
Reserved pineapple juice	$^1/_4$ cup	60 mL
Hot pepper jelly	1 tbsp.	15 mL
Low-sodium soy sauce	1 tbsp.	15 mL
Ground ginger	$^1/_2$ tsp.	2 mL
Small garlic clove, minced	1	1
Cornstarch	1 tsp.	5 mL
Canned pineapple slices, drained and juice reserved	14 oz.	398 mL
Hamburger buns	4	4
Light salad dressing (or mayonnaise)	2 tbsp.	30 mL
Hot pepper jelly (optional)	2 tbsp.	30 mL
Large lettuce leaves	4	4

Combine first amounts of soy sauce, reserved pineapple juice, garlic, and ginger in shallow glass casserole or pie plate. Stir in brown sugar. Makes $^1/_3$ cup (75 mL) marinade. ■ Coat chicken in marinade on each side. Cover. Marinate in refrigerator for 30 minutes or longer. Drain and discard marinade. ■ Combine second amount of reserved pineapple juice with next 5 ingredients in small saucepan. Cook and stir over medium-high until boiling and thickened. Makes $^1/_3$ cup (75 mL) sauce. ■ Preheat lightly sprayed electric grill to medium. Cook chicken on grill for 4 to 5 minutes per side, basting with sauce several times, until thoroughly cooked. Remove to plate. Cover or tent with foil to keep hot. ■ Grill pineapple slices, turning once and basting with sauce, until hot and glazed. Remove to plate. Discard any remaining sauce. ■ Toast buns, cut side down, until golden. Spread bottom halves with salad dressing. Spread top halves with second amount of jelly. Place lettuce on salad dressing. Lay chicken over lettuce. Top each with 2 pineapple slices. Replace tops of buns. Makes 4 large sandwiches.

1 sandwich: 402 Calories; 7.7 g Total Fat; 1105 mg Sodium; 33 g Protein; 50 g Carbohydrate; 2 g Dietary Fiber

Garden Patties

This patty requires gentle handling while turning. Great veggie tastes.

Cooked green lentils, drained	2 cups	500 mL
Grated zucchini, with peel	2 cups	500 mL
Finely grated carrot	$^1/_3$ cup	75 mL
Finely chopped green or red pepper	$^1/_3$ cup	75 mL
Finely chopped onion	2 tbsp.	30 mL
Finely chopped fresh sweet basil	2 tbsp.	30 mL
Garlic clove, minced	1	1
Seasoned salt	$^1/_2$ tsp.	2 mL
Freshly ground pepper, generous sprinkle		
Large eggs, fork-beaten	2	2
Fine dry bread crumbs	$^2/_3$ cup	150 mL

Preheat lightly sprayed electric grill to medium. Combine first 9 ingredients in medium bowl. ■ Add eggs. Mix well. Stir in bread crumbs. Form mixture into 6 patties. Cook on grill for 8 minutes. Carefully turn patties over. Cook for 5 to 8 minutes until firm and hot. Makes 6 patties.

1 patty: 170 Calories; 2.6 g Total Fat; 398 mg Sodium; 11 g Protein; 27 g Carbohydrate; 4 g Dietary Fiber

Variation: Add $^2/_3$ cup (150 mL) sharp Cheddar cheese to vegetable mixture before forming into patties.

Tuna Patties

The chili sauce takes this up a notch from a regular tuna fish sandwich.

Canned chunk light tuna, in water, drained	6 oz.	170 g
Coarse dry bread crumbs	$^1/_3$ cup	75 mL
Chili sauce	2 tbsp.	30 mL
Finely chopped celery	$^1/_4$ cup	60 mL
Thinly sliced green onion	2 tbsp.	30 mL
Chopped fresh parsley	1 tbsp.	15 mL
Freshly ground pepper, sprinkle		
Cayenne pepper, sprinkle (optional)		
Large egg, fork-beaten	1	1

(continued on next page)

Preheat lightly sprayed electric grill to medium. Combine all 9 ingredients in medium bowl. Let stand for 10 minutes for bread crumbs to absorb liquid. Form 2 patties, about 4 inches (10 cm) across. Cook patties on grill for 3 to 5 minutes per side until firm and hot. Makes 2 large patties.

1 patty: 236 Calories; 3.9 g Total Fat; 693 mg Sodium; 29 g Protein; 20 g Carbohydrate; 2 g Dietary Fiber

Bulgur Patties

Crunchy on the outside with lots of texture and color inside. Place in a toasted bun with the usual lettuce, tomato, mustard and ketchup. Pictured on page 90.

Bulgur wheat	**1 cup**	**250 mL**
Boiling water, to cover		
Finely shredded carrot	**$1/4$ cup**	**60 mL**
Finely shredded zucchini	**$1/4$ cup**	**60 mL**
Finely sliced green onion	**2 tbsp.**	**30 mL**
Chopped fresh parsley	**2 tbsp.**	**30 mL**
Ground walnuts	**2 tbsp.**	**30 mL**
Garlic clove, minced	**1**	**1**
Large eggs, fork-beaten	**2**	**2**
Hot pepper sauce	**1 tsp.**	**5 mL**
Salt	**1 tsp.**	**5 mL**
Freshly ground pepper, generous sprinkle		
Fresh whole wheat bread slices, processed into crumbs	**2**	**2**
Mashed potato (optional)	**$1/2$ cup**	**125 mL**
Canola oil	**1 tbsp.**	**15 mL**

Measure bulgur into medium bowl. Pour boiling water over to cover. Let stand for 30 minutes until most water is absorbed. Drain. ■ Add next 12 ingredients, 1 at a time, to bulgur, mixing after each addition. Let stand for 10 minutes for bread crumbs to absorb moisture. ■ Preheat lightly sprayed electric grill to medium-hot. Form bulgur mixture into 4 patties. Brush both sides of patties with oil. Cook on grill for 6 to 7 minutes per side until patties are browned and crispy. Makes 4 patties.

1 patty: 251 Calories; 8.3 g Total Fat; 795 mg Sodium; 10 g Protein; 37 g Carbohydrate; 8 g Dietary Fiber

Rice And Salmon Patties

Serve these eye-catching patties with Fresh Tartar Sauce, page 22, on the side. Pictured on page 36.

Cooked brown rice	2 cups	500 mL
Canned salmon, drained, skin and round bones removed, flaked	7¹/₂ oz.	213 g
Large eggs, fork-beaten	2	2
Coarse dry bread crumbs	1 cup	250 mL
Finely chopped red pepper	¹/₂ cup	125 mL
Finely chopped green onion	2 tbsp.	30 mL
Grated sharp Cheddar cheese	²/₃ cup	150 mL
Chopped fresh dill	1 tbsp.	15 mL
Freshly ground pepper, sprinkle		

Preheat lightly sprayed electric grill to medium. Combine all 9 ingredients in medium bowl. Divide into 4 portions. Form into flattened round patties. Cook on grill for 4 to 5 minutes per side until golden and firm. Makes 4 large patties.

1 patty: 423 Calories; 15.9 g Total Fat; 561 mg Sodium; 22 g Protein; 47 g Carbohydrate; 3 g Dietary Fiber

Mini Meal Patties

Bits of carrot show through. Somewhat like a meatloaf in a patty shape. Serve in a crusty bun with a salad for a full meal.

Whole wheat (or stoned wheat) crackers (approx. 12), processed into crumbs	²/₃ cup	150 mL
Large onion, cut into 8 chunks	1	1
Large carrot, cut into 1 inch (2.5 cm) pieces	1	1
Medium potato, peeled and cut into 8 chunks	1	1
Worcestershire sauce	2 tsp.	10 mL
Seasoned salt	1 tsp.	5 mL
Freshly ground pepper, sprinkle		
Large egg	1	1
Extra lean ground beef	12 oz.	340 g

(continued on next page)

Preheat lightly sprayed electric grill to medium-high. Pour cracker crumbs from processor or blender into large bowl. ■ Process next 7 ingredients, using pulsing motion, to finely chop vegetables. Pour over cracker crumbs in bowl. ■ Mix in ground beef until well blended. Form mixture into 8 thin patties. Cook on grill for 8 minutes per side, turning several times, until beef is cooked. Makes 8 patties.

1 patty: 122 Calories; 5.2 g Total Fat; 252 mg Sodium; 10 g Protein; 9 g Carbohydrate; 1 g Dietary Fiber

Turkey Patties

A lighter colored patty (which shows off the grill lines even better).

Lean ground white turkey	**1 lb.**	**454 g**
Fresh whole wheat bread slices, processed into crumbs	**2**	**2**
Finely chopped onion	**¹/₄ cup**	**60 mL**
Chopped fresh parsley	**¹/₄ cup**	**60 mL**
Chopped fresh marjoram (or oregano) leaves	**2 tbsp.**	**30 mL**
Salt	**1 tsp.**	**5 mL**
Freshly ground pepper, sprinkle		
Hot pepper sauce	**¹/₄ tsp.**	**1 mL**
Hot pepper jelly	**¹/₄ cup**	**60 mL**
Large egg	**1**	**1**
Hot pepper jelly	**2 tbsp.**	**30 mL**

Preheat lightly sprayed electric grill to medium. Combine first 10 ingredients in medium bowl. Divide mixture into 4 equal portions. Flatten each into 4 inch (10 cm) patty. ■ Stir second amount of jelly in small bowl until smooth. Warm gently in microwave if necessary. Cook patties on grill for 12 to 15 minutes, turning several times and basting with jelly on each side during last 2 minutes of cooking. Makes 4 patties.

1 patty: 237 Calories; 3.5 g Total Fat; 843 mg Sodium; 28 g Protein; 22 g Carbohydrate; 1 g Dietary Fiber

Mushroom Patties

Very moist and delicious! Very meaty, generous-sized patty with a definite mushroom flavor.

Extra lean ground beef	³/₄ lb.	340 g
Finely chopped onion	¹/₄ cup	60 mL
Chopped fresh brown mushrooms	2 cups	500 mL
Garlic clove, minced	1	1
Large egg, fork-beaten	1	1
Fresh whole wheat bread slices, processed into crumbs	2	2
Worcestershire sauce	2-4 tsp.	10-20 mL
Seasoned salt	1 tsp.	5 mL
Freshly ground pepper, sprinkle		
Grated Parmesan cheese (optional)	4 tsp.	20 mL

Preheat lightly sprayed electric grill to medium. Combine first 9 ingredients in medium bowl. Divide into 4 portions. Form each portion into 4 inch (10 cm) patty. Cook on grill for about 8 minutes per side until beef is no longer pink. ■ Sprinkle hot patties with 1 tsp. (5 mL) Parmesan cheese each. Makes 4 large patties.

1 patty: 199 Calories; 9.1 g Total Fat; 505 mg Sodium; 19 g Protein; 10 g Carbohydrate; 2 g Dietary Fiber

· ·

Clean the bottom tray and grease catcher of your electric grill after every use. Clean the lava rocks on your gas barbecue by turning them over carefully with tongs when the cooking is done but the gas is still on. Turn barbecue up to High and close the lid. Leave for about 15 minutes—then remember to turn off the barbecue! This will burn off the food bits that cause flare-ups. With a charcoal barbecue, line the bottom with heavy-duty foil before adding the briquettes. When the cooking is done and the barbecue and coals have cooled completely, simply gather up the foil and ash and throw away. This makes cleanup much easier, faster and more thorough.

Middle East Pitas

A more savory patty. The pita "pocket" holds the condiments well.

Lean ground lamb	$^3/_4$ lb.	340 g
Coarsely chopped onion	$^3/_4$ cup	175 mL
Garlic clove, halved	1	1
Coarsely chopped fresh parsley	2 tbsp.	30 mL
Coarsely chopped fresh mint leaves	1 tbsp.	15 mL
Large egg, fork-beaten	1	1
Salt	$^3/_4$ tsp.	4 mL
Ground cinnamon	$^1/_8$ tsp.	0.5 mL
Ground allspice	$^1/_{16}$ tsp.	0.5 mL
Freshly ground pepper, sprinkle		
Fine dry bread crumbs	$^1/_4$ cup	60 mL
Pita breads (4-5 inch, 10-12.5 cm, size)	6	6
Shredded lettuce	1 cup	250 mL
Diced tomato	$^1/_2$ cup	125 mL
Diced green pepper	$^1/_2$ cup	125 mL
Chopped mild onion	$^1/_3$ cup	75 mL
Herb Aioli, page 14 (or commercial Tahini sauce)	3 tbsp.	50 mL

Process first 10 ingredients in food processor until very soft and almost mushy. Cover. Chill overnight in refrigerator. ■ Divide into 12 portions, about 2 oz. (57 g) each. Roll each portion in bread crumbs. Form each portion into oval-shaped patties. Preheat lightly sprayed electric grill to medium. Cook patties on grill for about 15 minutes, carefully turning several times to brown well. ■ Fill each pita with 2 patties. ■ Divide lettuce, tomato, green pepper and second amount of onion among pitas. ■ Top each with 1$^1/_2$ tsp. (7 mL) Herb Aioli. Makes 6 stuffed pitas.

1 stuffed pita: 336 Calories; 12.3 g Total Fat; 702 mg Sodium; 15 g Protein; 41 g Carbohydrate; 1 g Dietary Fiber

Variation: Substitute large pitas with 12 mini (3 inch, 7.5 cm) pita breads. Use 1 patty in each and $^3/_4$ tsp. (4 mL) Herb Aioli. Makes 12.

Stuffed Pitas

A light tasty blend of vegetables that fits nicely into a mini pita "pocket" with the condiments.

Carrot, cut into 1 inch (2.5 cm) pieces	1	1
Garlic clove, minced (optional)	1	1
Green onion, cut into 2 inch (5 cm) pieces	1	1
Chopped celery	1/4 cup	60 mL
Fresh parsley sprig	1	1
Large egg	1	1
Ground white turkey	1/2 lb.	225 g
Fine dry bread crumbs	1/2 cup	125 mL
Seasoned salt	1/2 tsp.	2 mL
Freshly ground pepper, sprinkle		
Cranberry (or raspberry) jelly	2 tbsp.	30 mL
Small pita breads (3 inch, 7.5 cm, size)	7	7
Torn lettuce pieces	7	7
Diced tomato	1/3 cup	75 mL

Preheat lightly sprayed electric grill to medium. Place first 6 ingredients in food processor or blender. Process until almost smooth. ■ Combine well with turkey, bread crumbs, seasoned salt and pepper in medium bowl. Form into 14 flattened mini patties. ■ Cook patties on grill for 10 minutes, turning and basting with jelly, until cooked. ■ Insert 2 patties into each pita bread. ■ Add lettuce and tomato. Makes 7 stuffed pitas.

1 stuffed pita: 142 Calories; 1.9 g Total Fat; 247 mg Sodium; 11 g Protein; 20 g Carbohydrate; 1 g Dietary Fiber

1. Herbed Butter, page 22
2. Herbed Turkey Roll, page 60
3. Herbed Steak Slices, page 30
4. Stuffed Tenderloin, page 92

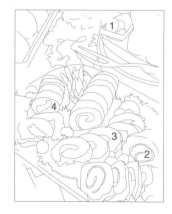

Pesto, Chicken And Pepper Pizza

Wonderful pesto and pepper flavor on this thick crusted pizza.

Boneless, skinless chicken breast halves (about 2)	**¹/₂ lb.**	**225 g**
Salt, sprinkle		
Freshly ground pepper, sprinkle		
Medium red pepper, halved and seeded	**¹/₂**	**¹/₂**
Olive oil	**2 tsp.**	**10 mL**
Focaccia bread (11 inch, 28 cm, size)	**1**	**1**
Basil pesto	**2 tbsp.**	**30 mL**
Grated asiago (or part-skim mozzarella) cheese	**¹/₃ cup**	**75 mL**
Grated Parmesan cheese	**1 tbsp.**	**15 mL**

Preheat barbecue to high. Sprinkle chicken breast with salt and pepper. ■ Place chicken and red pepper half, skin side down, on greased grill. Close lid. Cook for 8 to 10 minutes, turning chicken after 5 minutes but leaving pepper skin side down to blacken. Remove chicken. Cut into thin diagonal slices. Remove red pepper to bowl. Cover with plastic wrap until cool enough to handle. Peel off blackened skin and discard. Cut pepper into slivers. ■ Brush part of olive oil on bottom of focaccia. Combine remaining olive oil and pesto in small cup. Spread over top of focaccia to edges. Arrange chicken slices and red pepper slivers over pesto. Sprinkle both cheeses over top. Turn barbecue to medium. Place focaccia on greased grill. Cook for about 2 minutes until bottom is browned. Turn off heat but leave opposite burner on. Close lid. Let stand in warm barbecue for 5 minutes until cheese is melted. Cuts into 8 wedges.

1 wedge: 230 Calories; 4.6 g Total Fat; 386 mg Sodium; 13 g Protein; 33 g Carbohydrate; 1 g Dietary Fiber

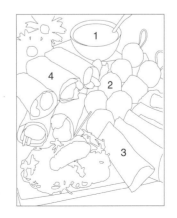

1. Japanese Ginger Sauce, page 20
2. Sesame Pork Balls, page 112
3. Crunchy Thai Wraps, page 57
4. Shanghai Wraps, page 56

Shanghai Wraps

Yummy moist patties tucked into a tortilla wrap. Pictured on page 54.

Lean ground pork	1 lb.	454 g
Fine dry bread crumbs	1/2 cup	125 mL
Large egg, fork-beaten	1	1
Finely sliced green onion	1/4 cup	60 mL
Finely chopped celery	1/4 cup	60 mL
Garlic cloves, minced	2	2
Low-sodium soy sauce	2 tbsp.	30 mL
Finely grated gingerroot	2 tsp.	10 mL
Cayenne pepper	1/4 tsp.	1 mL
Salt	1/8 tsp.	0.5 mL
Freshly ground pepper, sprinkle		
Canned whole baby corn, drained	14 oz.	398 mL
Flour tortillas (10 inch, 25 cm, size)	6	6
Hoisin sauce	2 tbsp.	30 mL
Green onions, slivered lengthwise	2	2
Grated carrot	1/3 cup	75 mL
Chopped fresh bean sprouts	1 cup	250 mL
Toasted sesame seeds (optional)	1 tbsp.	15 mL

Preheat lightly sprayed electric grill for 5 minutes to high. Combine first 11 ingredients in medium bowl. Divide into 6 equal portions. Form each portion into flattened patty or sausage shape. Place patties on grill. Cook for about 12 minutes, turning frequently, until no longer pink inside. ■ Cook corn on hot grill, turning several times, until heated through and slightly browned. ■ Sprinkle some water with fingers, on each tortilla. Stack damp tortillas on foil and enclose. Heat on grill for about 6 minutes, turning once, until warmed. ■ Spread center of each warm tortilla with 1 tsp. (5 mL) hoisin sauce. Place 1 patty and about 3 baby corn on each. Divide green onion, carrot, bean sprouts and sesame seeds over corn. Fold each into open-ended envelope or tuck 2 sides in, and tightly roll up. Makes 6 wraps.

1 wrap: 368 Calories; 6.4 g Total Fat; 1007 mg Sodium; 21 g Protein; 58 g Carbohydrate; 2 g Dietary Fiber

Crunchy Thai Wraps

For a different wrap with a nice crunchy texture, try these. Pictured on page 54.

Lime juice	4 tsp.	20 mL
Garlic clove, minced	1	1
Smooth peanut butter	2 tbsp.	30 mL
Dried crushed chilies	1/2 tsp.	2 mL
Granulated sugar	1/2 tsp.	2 mL
Canola oil	2 tbsp.	30 mL
Boneless, skinless chicken breast halves (about 2)	1/2 lb.	225 g
Fresh bean sprouts	2/3 cup	150 mL
Grated carrot	1/2 cup	125 mL
Green onions, sliced	2	2
Shredded lettuce, packed	2/3 cup	150 mL
Rice paper wrappers (8 inch, 20 cm, size)	4	4
Warm water, to cover		
Commercial peanut sauce	1/4 cup	60 mL

Preheat lightly sprayed electric grill for 5 minutes to medium. Combine first 6 ingredients in small bowl. Makes 6 tbsp. (100 mL) sauce. Divide sauce into 2 bowls. ■ Slash chicken breasts in 2 places. Place on grill. Baste both sides of chicken with sauce from first bowl. Discard any remaining sauce from that bowl. Cook for 8 to 10 minutes per side until no pink remains. Slice chicken breasts very thinly crosswise. Place in medium bowl. Pour sauce from second bowl over top. Toss gently. ■ Add bean sprouts, carrot, green onion and lettuce. Toss gently. ■ Soak rice papers in warm water in pie plate for 1 minute to soften. Lay on flat surface. Spoon 1/4 of chicken mixture across bottom 1/3 of each rice paper. ■ Drizzle 1/4 of commercial peanut sauce over chicken mixture on each. Fold up bottom and sides. Roll firmly. Makes 4 wraps.

1 wrap: 289 Calories; 16.8 g Total Fat; 379 mg Sodium; 19 g Protein; 17 g Carbohydrate; 2 g Dietary Fiber

....

It is so important to ensure that patties made with ground beef are cooked thoroughly so that no pink remains. A neat trick is to mix and form the patties and then poke your finger through the center of each to make a "doughnut". As the patty cooks, the hole will slowly close but will also ensure that the meat cooks in the center.

Quick Pizza

Can be served as a meal or great as an appetizer. Pictured on page 71.

Whole wheat (or regular) flour tortilla (10 inch, 25 cm, size)	1	1
Canola oil	1 tsp.	5 mL
Basil pesto	1 tbsp.	15 mL
Grated part-skim mozzarella cheese	1/3 cup	75 mL
Medium roma (plum) tomato, seeded and chopped	1	1
Finely chopped red (or other) mild onion	2 tbsp.	30 mL
Finely chopped green pepper	2 tbsp.	30 mL
Freshly ground pepper, sprinkle		

Preheat lightly sprayed electric grill for 5 minutes to medium-low. Brush 1 side of tortilla with oil. Place, oiled side down, on plate. ■ Spread with pesto. Sprinkle 1/2 of cheese over pesto. Layer tomato, red onion and green pepper over cheese. Sprinkle with pepper. Sprinkle with remaining 1/2 of cheese. Slide carefully onto grill. Cook for 5 minutes until tortilla is crispy and browned and cheese is melted. Cuts into 8 wedges.

1 wedge: 53 Calories; 2.3 g Total Fat; 81 mg Sodium; 2 g Protein; 6 g Carbohydrate; 1 g Dietary Fiber

Variation: Substitute sun-dried tomato pesto for basil pesto.

Grilled Quesadillas

Easy, fast and delicious with only a few ingredients.

Grated Monterey Jack cheese	1/2 cup	125 mL
Flour tortillas (10 inch, 25 cm, size)	2	2
Salsa (mild, medium or hot)	1/4 cup	60 mL
Chopped green onion	2 tsp.	10 mL
Finely diced red pepper	1 tbsp.	15 mL

(continued on next page)

Preheat lightly sprayed electric grill for 5 minutes to high. Sprinkle $^1/_2$ of cheese over 1 tortilla. Drizzle salsa over cheese. ■ Sprinkle with green onion and red pepper. Sprinkle with remaining cheese. Cover with second tortilla. Slide onto grill. Cook, uncovered, for 2 minutes. Carefully turn over. Cook for 2 to 3 minutes until cheese is melted and tortillas are crispy and browned. Cuts into 4 wedges each, for a total of 8 wedges.

1 wedge: 74 Calories; 2.5 g Total Fat; 214 mg Sodium; 3 g Protein; 9 g Carbohydrate; trace Dietary Fiber

Steak Donair

These make-at-home donairs are easy, as well as tasty using commonly stocked ingredients.

Top sirloin steak, trimmed of fat	$^3/_4$ **lb.**	**340 g**
Caesar dressing	**4 tbsp.**	**60 mL**
Pita breads (8 inch, 20 cm, size)	**4**	**4**
Medium onion, sliced	$^1/_2$	$^1/_2$
Large tomato, chopped	**1**	**1**
Shredded green lettuce, packed	$^1/_2$ **cup**	**125 mL**

Preheat lightly sprayed electric grill for 5 minutes to high. Place steak on grill for 30 seconds per side to sear. Baste with 1 tbsp. (15 mL) dressing. Cook for 5 to 6 minutes per side for medium rare doneness. Remove steak to plate. ■ Grill pitas on both sides until warmed. Thinly slice steak on diagonal across grain. Divide steak slices across center of each pita. ■ Sprinkle with onion, tomato and lettuce. Drizzle with remaining dressing. Roll pitas to enclose fillings. Makes 4 stuffed pitas.

1 stuffed pita: 394 Calories; 11.5 g Total Fat; 391 mg Sodium; 25 g Protein; 46 g Carbohydrate; 1 g Dietary Fiber

Chicken & Turkey

esides being a lean choice for daily protein requirements, poultry is so adaptable to many
exciting flavors. You can't go wrong choosing any of the recipes in this section! There
are even several that are appropriate for entertaining.

Herbed Turkey Roll

The oil and herb filling in this roll keeps the turkey moist all the way through. Pictured on page 53.

Turkey breast half (about 1¹/₂ lbs., 680 g)	**1**	**1**
Olive oil	**3 tbsp.**	**50 mL**
Garlic cloves, minced	**4**	**4**
Dijon mustard	**1 tbsp.**	**15 mL**
Chopped fresh parsley	**1 tbsp.**	**15 mL**
Chopped fresh chives	**1 tbsp.**	**15 mL**
Fresh rosemary leaves	**1-3 tsp.**	**5-15 mL**
Salt	**1 tsp.**	**5 mL**
Freshly ground pepper	**1 tsp.**	**5 mL**
Bacon slices	**3- 4**	**3- 4**

Preheat barbecue to medium. Butterfly turkey breast by cutting horizontally through
the middle, not quite to other side. Spread open and pound with smooth side of mallet
to thinner more even thickness. ■ Combine next 8 ingredients in small bowl. Spread
over flattened side of turkey breast. Roll tightly, starting from long edge. Tie with
butcher's string to secure. ■ Lay bacon slices over top. Carefully place on greased grill
over drip pan using indirect cooking method (see page 7). Close lid. Cook for about
1¹/₂ hours. Remove to platter and discard string. Discard bacon if desired. Slice into ³/₄
inch (2 cm) slices to serve.
Serves 4.

1 serving: 282 Calories; 11.6 g Total Fat; 801 mg Sodium; 41 g Protein; 2 g Carbohydrate; trace Dietary Fiber

Chicken With Garlic Sauce

You'll never do a chicken in the oven again. Remove the skin just before serving to lower the fat.

Whole chicken fryer	**3-3¹/₂ lbs.**	**1.4-1.6 kg**
Seasoned salt	**1 tsp.**	**5 mL**
Pepper	**¹/₄ tsp.**	**1 mL**
Whole garlic bulbs, with skins	**3**	**3**
White (or alcohol-free white) wine	**2 tbsp.**	**30 mL**
Water	**1 cup**	**250 mL**
Olive oil	**1 tbsp.**	**15 mL**
All-purpose flour	**1 tbsp.**	**15 mL**
Skim evaporated milk	**¹/₂ cup**	**125 mL**
Chicken bouillon powder	**1 tsp.**	**5 mL**
Chopped fresh parsley	**2 tbsp.**	**30 mL**

Preheat barbecue to medium. Wash chicken in cold water. Remove any parts from cavity and discard. Dry well inside and out with paper towels. Season inside of cavity with ¹/₄ tsp. (1 mL) seasoned salt and ¹/₈ tsp. (0.5 mL) pepper. Sprinkle remaining seasoned salt and pepper over outside of chicken. ■ Remove only loose papery skin from outside of garlic bulbs. Cut pointy end of garlic bulbs to expose most of individual cloves. Place inside chicken cavity. With butcher's string, tie up chicken legs to close cavity. Tie wings so they are close to body. Place chicken, breast side down, over drip pan, on greased grill, using indirect heat cooking method (see page 7). Close lid. Cook for 40 minutes. Turn chicken, breast side up. Cook for 50 to 60 minutes until chicken is done and juices run clear. ■ Untie chicken. Remove garlic bulbs. Cool bulbs enough to handle. Squeeze slightly softened bulbs over blender opening then drop in. Add wine and ¹/₂ cup (125 mL) water until almost smooth. ■ Heat olive oil in small saucepan. Stir in flour. Slowly add remaining ¹/₂ cup (125 mL) water. Slowly add evaporated milk, stirring constantly, until boiling and smooth. Stir in wine mixture, bouillon powder and parsley. Bring to a boil. Makes 2 cups (500 mL) sauce. Serve sauce with chicken. Serves 6.

1 serving: 423 Calories; 26.4 g Total Fat; 476 mg Sodium; 33 g Protein; 11 g Carbohydrate; 1 g Dietary Fiber

. . . .

Trim excess fat off meat before cooking. This will prevent flare-ups and burning and will allow the meat to brown evenly to obtain the more professional and visually-appealing grill lines.

Orange Chicken

The orange slices make a wonderful presentation on a serving platter. Serve this with wild rice.

Prepared orange juice	$1/4$ **cup**	**60 mL**
Garlic cloves, minced	**2**	**2**
Olive oil	**2 tbsp.**	**30 mL**
Finely grated gingerroot	**1 tbsp.**	**15 mL**
Lemon pepper	$1/2$ **tsp.**	**2 mL**
Boneless, skinless chicken breast halves (about 1 lb., 454 g)	**4**	**4**
Orange marmalade	$1/4$ **cup**	**60 mL**
Prepared orange juice	**2 tbsp.**	**30 mL**
Large oranges, peeled and cut into $1/2$ **inch (12 mm) slices**	**2**	**2**

Preheat lightly sprayed electric grill to medium-high. Combine first 5 ingredients in shallow glass casserole or pie plate. Makes $1/4$ cup (60 mL) marinade. ■ Marinate chicken breasts in mixture at room temperature for about 15 minutes. Drain and discard marinade. Place chicken on grill. Cook for 10 minutes per side. ■ Warm marmalade and orange juice in small saucepan. Brush over chicken breasts on each side. Grill for 2 minutes per side. Remove to plate and cover with foil. ■ Cook orange slices for 2 minutes, turning and brushing with remaining marmalade mixture several times, until hot and glazed. Arrange orange slices over chicken on serving plate. Serves 4.

1 serving: 311 Calories; 9.5 g Total Fat; 67 mg Sodium; 28 g Protein; 29 g Carbohydrate; 3 g Dietary Fiber

Chicken In Yogurt

A hint of almond blends in so delicately with the exotic spices.

Plain low-fat yogurt	$1/2$ **cup**	**125 mL**
Lemon juice	**2 tbsp.**	**30 mL**
Garlic cloves, minced	**2**	**2**
Salt	**1 tsp.**	**5 mL**
Ground ginger	**1 tsp.**	**5 mL**
Ground cumin	**1 tsp.**	**5 mL**
Paprika	**1 tsp.**	**5 mL**
Almond flavoring	**1 tsp.**	**5 mL**
Chicken pieces, skinned, bone in	**2 lbs.**	**900 g**

(continued on next page)

Combine first 8 ingredients in small bowl. Makes $^2/_3$ cup (150 mL) marinade. ■ Place chicken pieces in sealable plastic bag or shallow casserole. Pour marinade over chicken. Seal bag. Marinate in refrigerator for at least 4 hours or overnight. Drain and discard marinade. Preheat barbecue to medium. Place chicken on greased grill. Close lid. Cook chicken for 5 minutes, turning 2 to 3 times, until browned. Turn off burner under chicken, leaving other burner on high. Close lid. Cook chicken pieces for 15 to 20 minutes until chicken is well done. Serves 4.

1 serving: 150 Calories; 3.6 g Total Fat; 613 mg Sodium; 25 g Protein; 3 g Carbohydrate; trace Dietary Fiber

Lemon Chicken And Sauce

The sauce takes on a pretty pink color from the grenadine. Don't forget to eat the lettuce—it's deliciously refreshing with lemon sauce on it!

Frozen lemonade concentrate, thawed	**$^1/_4$ cup**	**60 mL**
Canola oil	**1 tbsp.**	**15 mL**
Grenadine syrup	**1 tbsp.**	**15 mL**
Onion powder	**$^1/_2$ tsp.**	**2 mL**
Garlic salt	**$^1/_2$ tsp.**	**2 mL**
Boneless, skinless chicken breast halves (about 4)	**1 lb.**	**454 g**
Frozen lemonade concentrate, thawed	**$^1/_4$ cup**	**60 mL**
Water	**$^1/_2$ cup**	**125 mL**
Grenadine syrup	**2 tbsp.**	**30 mL**
Cornstarch	**1 tbsp.**	**15 mL**
Finely grated lemon peel	**1 tsp.**	**5 mL**
Crisp iceberg lettuce, shredded	**2 cups**	**500 mL**
Lemon slices, for garnish		

Combine first 5 ingredients in small bowl. Makes about $^1/_3$ cup (75 mL) marinade. ■ Place chicken in sealable plastic bag. Pour marinade over chicken. Seal bag. Marinate in refrigerator for several hours or overnight. Drain and discard marinade. Preheat barbecue to medium. Place chicken on greased grill. Close lid. Cook for 20 to 25 minutes, turning several times to prevent overbrowning. ■ Combine next 5 ingredients in small saucepan. Boil until thickened. Makes about $^2/_3$ cup (150 mL) sauce. ■ Divide lettuce among 4 dinner plates. Place chicken on lettuce. Serve sauce over chicken. ■ Garnish with lemon slices. Serves 4.

1 serving: 295 Calories; 6.4 g Total Fat; 235 mg Sodium; 27 g Protein; 32 g Carbohydrate; trace Dietary Fiber

Chicken Nibbles

Present these inserted with decorative picks.

Lean ground chicken (white meat)	**1 lb.**	**454 g**
Large egg, fork-beaten	**1**	**1**
Salted soda crackers, processed into fine crumbs	**16**	**16**
Low-sodium soy sauce	**2 tbsp.**	**30 mL**
Sake (rice wine) or dry sherry	**2 tbsp.**	**30 mL**
Finely grated gingerroot	**1 tbsp.**	**15 mL**
Golden corn syrup	**3 tbsp.**	**50 mL**
Low-sodium soy sauce	**1 tbsp.**	**15 mL**
Sherry (or alcohol-free sherry)	**2 tbsp.**	**30 mL**
Cayenne pepper	**$1/_{16}$ tsp.**	**0.5 mL**

Preheat lightly sprayed electric grill to high. Combine first 6 ingredients in medium bowl. Form into small $1^1/_2$ inch (3.8 cm) balls, using rounded $1/_2$ tbsp. (7 mL) per ball. Cook balls on grill for 10 to 15 minutes, turning and moving several times, until browned. ■ Combine remaining 4 ingredients in small dish. Makes $1/_3$ cup (75 mL) basting sauce. Baste meatballs with sauce. Cook for about 5 minutes, turning and basting several times, until chicken is no longer pink. Discard any remaining sauce. Makes 30 meatballs.

2 meatballs: 70 Calories; 1.3 g Total Fat; 186 mg Sodium; 8 g Protein; 6 g Carbohydrate; trace Dietary Fiber

Variation: Soak 4 inch (10 cm) bamboo skewers in water for 10 minutes. Skewer 2 balls on each skewer. Cook skewers on greased hot grill for 10 to 15 minutes, turning several times. Brush with corn syrup mixture turning several times, for 5 minutes until chicken is cooked. Makes 15 skewers.

Quick Turkey Cutlets

Experiment with any low-fat dressing you have in your refrigerator to replace the creamy cucumber.

Turkey breast cutlets (about $1/_2$ lb., 225 g)	**2**	**2**
Salt, sprinkle		
Lemon pepper, sprinkle		
Low-fat creamy cucumber dressing	**2 tbsp.**	**30 mL**
Light mayonnaise	**2 tbsp.**	**30 mL**
Small garlic clove, minced	**1**	**1**
Chopped fresh oregano leaves (or $1/_8$ tsp., 0.5 mL, dried)	**$1/_2$ tsp.**	**2 mL**
Turmeric	**$1/_4$ tsp.**	**1 mL**

(continued on next page)

Preheat lightly sprayed electric grill to medium-low. Season cutlets with salt and lemon pepper. ■ Combine remaining 5 ingredients in small bowl. Makes 1/4 cup (60 mL) basting sauce. Cook turkey cutlets on grill for about 15 minutes, basting with sauce several times and turning frequently so they don't burn, until juices run clear and meat is no longer pink. Serves 2.

1 serving: 276 Calories; 19.3 g Total Fat; 272 mg Sodium; 20 g Protein; 4 g Carbohydrate; trace Dietary Fiber

Chutney Chicken

Slightly precooking the chicken pieces in the microwave makes for quicker cooking on the barbecue.

Chicken pieces, skinned, bone in (about 8)	**1³/₄ lbs.**	**790 g**
Water	**2 tbsp.**	**30 mL**
Lemon pepper	**1 tsp.**	**5 mL**
Mango chutney, large pieces chopped fine	**²/₃ cup**	**150 mL**
Hot water	**2 tbsp.**	**30 mL**
Ground ginger	**1 tsp.**	**5 mL**

Arrange chicken in single layer in greased small shallow roaster or casserole. Sprinkle with water. Bake, covered, in 400°F (205°C) oven for 30 minutes. Drain any liquid. Sprinkle chicken pieces with lemon pepper. (Or arrange chicken in microwave-safe shallow casserole, with meatiest portions turned to outside of dish. Omit water. Cover with waxed paper. Microwave on medium-high (75%) for 15 minutes. Drain liquid. Season chicken with lemon pepper.) ■ Process remaining 3 ingredients in blender until smooth. Makes ²/₃ cup (150 mL) basting sauce. Preheat barbecue to medium. Place chicken on greased grill. Close lid. Cook for 20 minutes, turning and basting with sauce several times, until chicken is cooked. Discard any remaining sauce. Makes 8 to 10 pieces, enough for 4 servings.

1 serving: 96 Calories; 1.3 g Total Fat; 33 mg Sodium; 9 g Protein; 12 g Carbohydrate; trace Dietary Fiber

Devilish Wings

The hot sauce can be reduced to one or two tablespoons if you're not brave enough to serve these as is! Nice garlic aftertaste.

Prepared orange juice	**¹/₃ cup**	**75 mL**
Cornstarch	**2 tsp.**	**10 mL**
Low-sodium soy sauce	**¹/₃ cup**	**75 mL**
Dry mustard	**³/₄ tsp.**	**4 mL**
Commercial hot sauce (not Tabasco)	**3 tbsp.**	**50 mL**
Garlic cloves, minced	**4**	**4**
Chicken wings, tips removed (about 12)	**2 lbs.**	**900 g**

Preheat barbecue to medium-low. Combine first 6 ingredients in small saucepan. Bring to a boil, stirring frequently, until slightly thickened. Makes about ³/₄ cup (175 mL) basting sauce. ■ Place wings on greased grill. Close lid. Cook chicken for about 30 minutes, turning and basting liberally with sauce, until cooked and glazed. Discard any remaining sauce. Makes about 12 wings.

2 glazed wings: 218 Calories; 13.4 g Total Fat; 489 mg Sodium; 20 g Protein; 4 g Carbohydrate; trace Dietary Fiber

Honey Lemon Wings

Wings can be pushed onto double-pronged skewers for easier turning if desired.

Lemon juice	**¹/₄ cup**	**60 mL**
Low-sodium soy sauce	**¹/₄ cup**	**60 mL**
Cornstarch	**2 tsp.**	**10 mL**
Finely grated gingerroot	**2 tsp.**	**10 mL**
Garlic cloves, minced	**4**	**4**
Liquid honey	**¹/₄ cup**	**60 mL**
Ketchup	**2 tbsp.**	**30 mL**
Chicken wings, tips removed (about 12)	**2 lbs.**	**900 g**

Combine first 7 ingredients in small saucepan. Bring to a boil, stirring often, until slightly thickened. Makes about ³/₄ cup (175 mL) basting sauce. ■ Preheat barbecue to low. Place wings on greased grill. Close lid. Cook for about 20 minutes, turning and basting frequently with sauce. Cook for 10 to 15 minutes, until glazed and no pink remains. Discard any remaining sauce. Makes about 12 wings.

2 glazed wings: 255 Calories; 13.3 g Total Fat; 438 mg Sodium; 20 g Protein; 14 g Carbohydrate; trace Dietary Fiber

Fish

Learn to love fish all over again with the tasty choices you'll find in this section. Besides being delicious, these recipes are quick and easy. Whether you choose whole fish, fillets or steaks, little preparation is required. Fish is naturally tender so it does not need to marinate longer than about 15 minutes. Cooking time is very quick too, so be sure to have salads and vegetable accompaniments ready to serve.

Far East Snapper

Hint of five-spice seasoning gives a glimpse into far away exotic places.

Tomato sauce	**¹/₂ cup**	**125 mL**
Lemon juice	**3 tbsp.**	**50 mL**
Low-sodium soy sauce	**3 tbsp.**	**50 mL**
Canola oil	**1 tbsp.**	**15 mL**
Chinese five-spice seasoning	**1 tsp.**	**5 mL**
Snapper fillets, skin removed	**1¹/₄ lbs.**	**560 g**

Combine first 5 ingredients in small bowl. Makes about 1 cup (250 mL) marinade.
■ Lay fillets flat in shallow glass pie plate or casserole. Pour marinade over fish. Cover. Marinate in refrigerator for at least 1 to 1¹/₂ hours. Drain and discard marinade. Preheat lightly sprayed electric grill to medium-high. Place fillets on grill. Cook for 5 to 6 minutes per side until fish is opaque and flakes easily with fork. Serves 4.

1 serving: 181 Calories; 4.5 g Total Fat; 566 mg Sodium; 30 g Protein; 4 g Carbohydrate; trace Dietary Fiber

Grilled Snapper

The tangy dressing with a hint of dill complements the snapper nicely.

Light salad dressing (or mayonnaise)	**4 tbsp.**	**60 mL**
Dijon mustard	**2-3 tsp.**	**10-15 mL**
Chopped fresh dill (or 1 tsp., 5 mL, dried)	**4 tsp.**	**20 mL**
Finely chopped fresh chives (or 1 tsp., 5 mL, dried)	**4 tsp.**	**20 mL**
Snapper fillets	**1¹/₄ lbs.**	**560 g**

Preheat lightly greased electric grill to medium-high. Combine first 4 ingredients in small bowl. ■ Spread mixture over top side of fillets. Lay, skin side or firm side down, on greased grill for 12 to 14 minutes, without turning, until fish is opaque and flakes easily with fork. Serves 4.

1 serving: 191 Calories; 6.1 g Total Fat; 224 mg Sodium; 29 g Protein; 3 g Carbohydrate; trace Dietary Fiber

Dill-Buttered Salmon

Dill and salmon just seem to go together. Simple, delicious—enough said!

Tub margarine (or hard margarine, softened)	**¹/₄ cup**	**60 mL**
Lemon pepper	**1 tsp.**	**5 mL**
Chopped fresh dill (or 2¹/₂ tsp., 12 mL, dried)	**3 tbsp.**	**50 mL**
Salmon steaks (about 6 oz., 170 g, each)	**4**	**4**

Preheat barbecue to high. Combine margarine, lemon pepper and dill in small bowl. ■ Cook salmon on greased grill for 1 minute. Turn. Spread grilled side with margarine mixture. Close lid. Cook for 8 to 10 minutes until fish is opaque and flakes easily with fork. Serves 4.

1 serving: 278 Calories; 16.7 g Total Fat; 241 mg Sodium; 32 g Protein; 1 g Carbohydrate; trace Dietary Fiber

Basted Mini Salmon Rolls

An interesting way to present salmon. Serves 4 as a first course or 2 as an entrée. Serve with
Blended Pepper Coulis, page 12. Pictured on back cover.

Salmon steaks (about 6 oz., 170 g, each)	**2**	**2**
Tub margarine	**2 tbsp.**	**30 mL**
Freshly squeezed lemon juice	**4 tsp.**	**20 mL**
Finely grated lemon peel	**1 tsp.**	**5 mL**
Chopped fresh parsley	**2 tbsp.**	**30 mL**
Salt	**¹/₂ tsp.**	**2 mL**
Freshly ground pepper, sprinkle		

Preheat lightly sprayed electric grill to medium-high. **1.** Cut around bone in salmon
steaks. Remove. **2.** Cut through joined part of steaks to make 4 long narrow pieces.
Pull out any other visible bones using tweezers. Place 1 salmon piece on cutting
board. Insert very sharp knife between skin and flesh. Cut away skin, keeping knife as
close as possible to skin. Repeat with other pieces. Discard skins. **3.** Curl each piece
into a round, wrapping thinner part around thicker end. Tie with butcher's string to
hold round shape. ■ Melt margarine in small saucepan. Stir in lemon juice, lemon
peel, parsley, salt and pepper. Baste both sides of rolls. Place on grill. Cook for about
10 minutes, turning and basting frequently with lemon butter, until salmon flakes
easily with fork. Makes 4 rolls.

1 roll: 137 Calories; 8.1 g Total Fat; 456 mg Sodium; 16 g Protein; 1 g Carbohydrate; trace Dietary Fiber

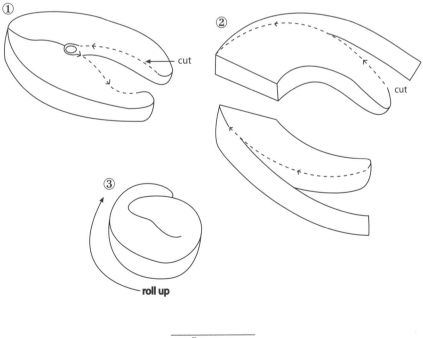

Salmon Fillets With Walnut Pesto

The sweet flavor of salmon is complemented by an amazing walnut and dill combination.

WALNUT PESTO		
Olive oil	1 tbsp.	15 mL
Walnut oil	1 tbsp.	15 mL
Walnut pieces	2 tbsp.	30 mL
Chopped fresh parsley	2 tbsp.	30 mL
Chopped fresh dill	1 tbsp.	15 mL
Lemon juice	2 tsp.	10 mL
Garlic clove, minced	1	1
Grated Parmesan cheese	1 tbsp.	15 mL
Salt	$^1/_4$ tsp.	1 mL
Freshly ground pepper, sprinkle		
Salmon fillets, with skin (about 2)	$1^1/_2$ lbs.	680 g

Walnut Pesto: Combine first 8 ingredients in blender or food processor. Process until finely chopped. ■ Stir in salt and pepper. Makes $^1/_3$ cup (75 mL) pesto. ■ Place salmon fillets, skin side down, on plate. Spread $^1/_2$ of pesto on flesh of each fillet. Cover. Marinate in refrigerator for 1 hour. Preheat barbecue to medium-high. Place fillets, skin side down, on greased grill. Close lid. Cook for 8 to 10 minutes until salmon flakes easily with fork but is still moist. Cut or lift salmon flesh off skin to serve. Serves 4.

1 serving: 258 Calories; 13.9 g Total Fat; 279 mg Sodium; 33 g Protein; 1 g Carbohydrate; trace Dietary Fiber

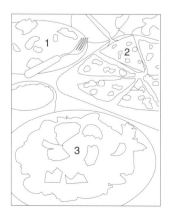

1. Stirless Stir-Fry, page 130
2. Quick Pizza, page 58
3. Chorizo And Rotini Dinner, page 88

Halibut With Mango Salsa

A ripe juicy mango is essential for this salsa as the juices provide a touch of sweetness. Pictured on page 17.

MANGO SALSA

Ripe large mango, diced (see Tip, page 13)	**1**	**1**
Medium English cucumber, with peel, cut into ¹/₂ inch (12 mm) cubes	**¹/₂**	**¹/₂**
Chopped red onion	**¹/₂ cup**	**125 mL**
Green jalapeño pepper, seeded and finely chopped (see Note)	**1**	**1**
Lime juice	**2 tbsp.**	**30 mL**
Chopped fresh cilantro (optional)	**2 tbsp.**	**30 mL**
Salt	**¹/₂ tsp.**	**2 mL**
Freshly ground pepper, sprinkle		
Halibut steaks (about 6 oz., 170 g, each)	**4**	**4**
Lemon pepper, sprinkle		

Mango Salsa: Combine first 8 ingredients in medium bowl. Cover. Let stand at room temperature for 1 hour to meld flavors and form juices. Makes 2¹/₃ cups (575 mL) salsa. ■ Season halibut steaks on both sides with lemon pepper. Preheat lightly sprayed electric grill to high. Cook fish on grill for 3 to 4 minutes per side until fish flakes easily with fork. Place on plate. Spoon salsa over top. Serves 4.

1 serving: 241 Calories; 4.2 g Total Fat; 434 mg Sodium; 36 g Protein; 14 g Carbohydrate; 2 g Dietary Fiber

Note: When chopping hot peppers use gloves, as the caustic oily compounds, called capsaicin (kap-SAY-ih-sihn), permeate the skin and can cause a burning sensation.

1. Fresh Fruit Quesadillas, page 78
2. Sweet-Filled Apples, page 134
3. Grilled Brie And Fruit Crostini, page 76

Fruit

from appetizers and accompaniments to snacks and desserts—fruits play a big role in a healthy diet. Flavors have not been compromised in our efforts to keep fat to a minimum in the following recipes. In fact, grilling is an excellent way to bring out the sweet, ripe flavors of most fruits. As the heat cools down after grilling the main meal, this is an ideal time to cook slices of fresh fruits. Enjoy a variety of in-season fruits straight off the grill.

Margaritagrill

Do this with friends sitting around a table on the deck or patio. Serve with cheese on the side.
Pictured on page 89.

Tequila	**¹/₄ cup**	**60 mL**
Orange-flavored liqueur (such as Triple Sec or Grand Marnier)	**¹/₄ cup**	**60 mL**
Freshly squeezed lemon juice	**1 tbsp.**	**15 mL**
Finely grated lemon peel	**1 tsp.**	**5 mL**
Freshly squeezed lime juice	**1 tbsp.**	**15 mL**
Finely grated lime peel	**1 tsp.**	**5 mL**
Brown sugar, packed	**¹/₄ cup**	**60 mL**
Slightly green bananas, cut into slices on diagonal	**2**	**2**
Medium apple, cored and sliced into rings	**1**	**1**
Large orange, peeled and sliced crosswise	**1**	**1**
Medium nectarines (or peaches, stones removed), cut into 6 wedges each	**2**	**2**

Preheat lightly sprayed electric grill to high. Stir first 7 ingredients together in small bowl until brown sugar is dissolved. Makes ³/₄ cup (175 mL) marinade. ■ Toss fruit with marinade in large bowl. Marinate at room temperature for 30 minutes. Drain and discard marinade. Cook fruit on grill for about 1 minute per side. Serves 6.

1 serving: 132 Calories; 0.5 g Total Fat; 2 mg Sodium; 1 g Protein; 28 g Carbohydrate; 2 g Dietary Fiber

Tropical Grilled Dessert

The flavors permeate the pineapple rings.

Dark (or amber) rum	**¹/₄ cup**	**60 mL**
Brown sugar, packed	**¹/₄ cup**	**60 mL**
Vanilla	**¹/₂ tsp.**	**2 mL**
Fresh pineapple, peeled, cored and cut into 1 inch (2.5 cm) thick rings	**1**	**1**

Combine rum, brown sugar and vanilla in small bowl. Stir to dissolve brown sugar. Makes ¹/₂ cup (125 mL) marinade. Pour into shallow glass dish or casserole. ■ Lay pineapple rings in marinade. Marinate at room temperature for 15 minutes. Turn rings over. Marinate for 15 minutes. Preheat lightly sprayed electric grill to medium-high. Drain and reserve marinade. Place rings on grill. Cook for 8 to 10 minutes, turning and basting with leftover marinade, until hot and golden. Discard any remaining marinade. Makes 6 glazed rings.

1 glazed ring: 107 Calories; 0.5 g Total Fat; 4 mg Sodium; trace Protein; 22 g Carbohydrate; 1 g Dietary Fiber

Rum Pineapple

First a burst of pineapple, then the lingering flavor of rum. Picturesque accompaniment for grilled ham steaks.

Dark rum	**¹/₃ cup**	**75 mL**
Liquid honey	**¹/₃ cup**	**75 mL**
Fresh pineapple, peeled, cored and cut into ³/₄ inch (2 cm) thick rings	**1**	**1**

Preheat barbecue to medium-high. Combine rum and honey in small bowl. Makes ²/₃ cup (150 mL) basting sauce. ■ Place pineapple rings on greased grill. Close lid. Cook for 10 minutes, turning and basting with sauce several times, until rings are golden and glazed. Discard any remaining sauce. Makes 8 glazed rings.

1 glazed ring: 95 Calories; 0.4 g Total Fat; 2 mg Sodium; trace Protein; 20 g Carbohydrate; 1 g Dietary Fiber

Grilled Brie And Fruit Crostini

What an impressive appetizer— summer or winter! Use the fruit salsa as an accompaniment for fish, chicken or pork as well. Pictured on page 72.

FRUITY SALSA

Diced mango	¹/₂ cup	125 mL
Diced red apple, with peel	¹/₂ cup	125 mL
White kidney beans, drained, rinsed and coarsely chopped	¹/₂ cup	125 mL
Finely chopped red onion	2 tbsp.	30 mL
Small hot pepper, seeded and diced very fine (see Note), optional	1	1
Balsamic vinegar	2 tbsp.	30 mL
Granulated sugar	1 tsp.	5 mL
Chopped fresh parsley	1 tbsp.	15 mL
Chopped fresh cilantro	1 tbsp.	15 mL
Baguette slices, cut ¹/₂ inch (12 mm) thick	24	24
Small Brie cheese rounds, with rind	2 × 4 oz.	2 × 125 g
Olive oil	¹/₄ cup	60 mL

Fruity Salsa: Combine first 9 ingredients in small bowl. Cover. Let stand at room temperature for 1 hour, stirring several times, for flavors to meld. Makes 2 cups (500 mL) salsa. ■ Preheat lightly sprayed electric grill to medium. Lightly brush baguette slices and Brie rounds with olive oil on both sides. Place baguette slices on grill. Cook for about 1 minute until toasted on both sides. Increase heat to medium-high. Place both Brie rounds on grill. Cook for 4 to 5 minutes on each side, turning carefully, until soft to touch. Serve with salsa. Makes 24 appetizer servings.

1 serving: 140 Calories; 6.1 g Total Fat; 211 mg Sodium; 5 g Protein; 16 g Carbohydrate; 1 g Dietary Fiber

Note: When chopping hot peppers use gloves, as the caustic oily compounds, called capsaicin (kap-SAY-ih-sihn), permeate the skin and can cause a burning sensation.

....

Grill slices of sweet breads, such as brioche, scones or raisin bread, to accompany grilled fruit. Sprinkle both fruit and bread with cinnamon for the final touch.

Apple And Cheese Pizza

A very pretty presentation for dessert. Try it for brunch or lunch too! Pictured on page 89.

All-purpose flour	**1 cup**	**250 mL**
Whole wheat flour	**1/2 cup**	**125 mL**
Instant yeast	**1 1/2 tsp.**	**7 mL**
Salt	**1/2 tsp.**	**2 mL**
Granulated sugar	**1/4 tsp.**	**1 mL**
Ground cinnamon	**1/8-1/4 tsp.**	**0.5-1 mL**
Canola oil	**2 tbsp.**	**30 mL**
Very warm water	**1/2 cup**	**125 mL**
Red apples, with peel, cored and thinly sliced	**2**	**2**
Lemon juice	**1/2 cup**	**125 mL**
Grated sharp Cheddar cheese	**1 cup**	**250 mL**
Brown sugar, packed	**1/4 cup**	**60 mL**

Measure first 6 ingredients into food processor. Process briefly to combine. ■ Pour oil and very warm water through opening in lid while processing, until dough starts to form a ball. Knead 4 or 5 times on lightly floured surface. Cover. Let rest in warm place for 15 minutes. Divide ball into 4 equal portions. Pat or roll out each into thin 7 inch (18 cm) circle. Cover. ■ Measure apple into medium bowl. Let stand in lemon juice until ready to use. ■ Preheat lightly sprayed electric grill to high. Place 1 crust on grill. Cover with large saucepan lid. Cook each crust for 2 to 3 minutes until bottom is crisp and "spotty." Turn over. Cover browned sides with cheese. Drain apple and blot dry. Divide and arrange over cheese. Sprinkle each with about 1 tbsp. (15 mL) brown sugar. Cover with lid. Cook for 2 to 3 minutes until cheese is melted and bottom of crust is browned. Makes 4 pizzas.

1 pizza: 465 Calories; 17.7 g Total Fat; 531 mg Sodium; 14 g Protein; 66 g Carbohydrate; 5 g Dietary Fiber

....

The outer edges of a gas or charcoal barbecue tend to be cooler than the inner area. Use these different heat zones to your advantage. Place foods that require more gentle heat, such as fruits and vegetables, in the cooler area to prevent overcooking.

Fresh Fruit Quesadillas

Almost like a Danish pastry, without all the calories! Creamy texture inside. Good with mashed banana instead of apple. Pictured on page 72.

Light cream cheese, softened	4 oz.	125 g
Brown sugar, packed	2 tbsp.	30 mL
Vanilla	$1/_2$ tsp.	2 mL
Flour tortillas (10 inch, 25 cm, size)	4	4
Finely diced red apple, with peel	1 cup	250 mL
Ground cinnamon, sprinkle		

Preheat lightly sprayed electric grill to medium-low. Combine cream cheese, brown sugar and vanilla in small bowl until smooth. ■ Divide and spread mixture over 2 tortillas. ■ Sprinkle apple over remaining 2 tortillas. Sprinkle apple with cinnamon. Cover with first 2 tortillas. Slide, apple side down, onto grill. Cook for $1^1/_2$ to 2 minutes. Carefully turn over. Cook for $1^1/_2$ to 2 minutes until crispy and browned. Let stand for 1 minute. Cuts into 4 wedges each, for a total of 8.

1 wedge: 137 Calories; 3 g Total Fat; 252 mg Sodium; 5 g Protein; 23 g Carbohydrate; trace Dietary Fiber

Peach Flambé à la Barbecue

Serve a dollop of whipped cream or ice cream in the center of each peach.

Peaches, cut in half and stones discarded	2	2
Hard margarine (or butter), melted	2 tsp.	10 mL
Granulated sugar	$1/_2$ tsp.	2 mL
Grand Marnier liqueur (or Peach Schnapps)	4 tsp.	20 mL
Grand Marnier liqueur (or Peach Schnapps), warmed in microwave for 10 seconds	2 tsp.	10 mL

Preheat barbecue to high. Poke fork into peach flesh in several places. Do not pierce skin. Brush cut surface of peach with melted margarine. Place, cut side down, on greased grill for 1 minute or just until warm and grill marks are evident. ■ Turn, cut side up, and lightly sprinkle with sugar. Pour about 1 tsp. (5 mL) liqueur into each peach cavity. Cook for 1 minute. Remove peaches to serving plate. Take immediately to table. ■ Drizzle each with about $1/_2$ tsp. (2 mL) liqueur. Light. Makes 4 peach halves.

1 peach half: 69 Calories; 2 g Total Fat; 23 mg Sodium; trace Protein; 9 g Carbohydrate; 1 g Dietary Fiber

Pear And Cheese Wedges

Serve the wedges on individual dessert plates with a knife and fork. A light, just right ending to any meal.

Part-skim ricotta cheese	**1¹/₃ cups**	**325 mL**
Brown sugar, packed	**2 tbsp.**	**30 mL**
Vanilla	**¹/₂ tsp.**	**2 mL**
Ground cinnamon, sprinkle		
Whole wheat tortillas (10 inch, 25 cm, size)	**4**	**4**
Canned pears, drained, sliced into thin wedges	**14 oz.**	**398 mL**
Ground nutmeg, sprinkle (optional)		

Preheat lightly sprayed electric grill to medium-low. Combine ricotta cheese, brown sugar, vanilla and cinnamon in small bowl. ■ Divide and spread mixture over 2 tortillas. ■ Arrange drained pears on remaining 2 tortillas. Sprinkle with nutmeg. Cover with first 2 tortillas. Slide, pear side down, onto grill. Cook for 1¹/₂ to 2 minutes until crispy and browned. Let stand for 1 minute. Cut each into 4 wedges, for a total of 8.

1 wedge: 223 Calories; 4.9 g Total Fat; 353 mg Sodium; 10 g Protein; 37 g Carbohydrate; 4 g Dietary Fiber

Marinades & Basting Sauces

angy marinades and sweet basting sauces bring grilled foods to life. You can marinate almost any meat, poultry or fish to boost or delicately alter the flavor, or in some cases, to help tenderize. Even vegetables benefit from a short soaking time in a tasty marinade. Soy sauce and lemon juice are popular for just about any marinade base. Fresh ginger is nice with beef. Dill is the perfect herb for salmon, and garlic goes with just about anything! For additional tips and information, read Marinating Magic on page 10.

Beer Sauce

Use this rich-looking sauce for brushing on ribs, steaks or burgers during the last few minutes of grilling. Will keep covered for two to three weeks in the refrigerator.

Commercial barbecue sauce	**1 cup**	**250 mL**
Ketchup	**$^1/_2$ cup**	**125 mL**
Beer	**$^2/_3$ cup**	**150 mL**
Finely chopped onion	**$^1/_2$ cup**	**125 mL**
Liquid honey	**2 tbsp.**	**30 mL**
Worcestershire sauce	**4 tsp.**	**20 mL**
Dijon mustard	**4 tsp.**	**20 mL**
Garlic cloves, minced	**2**	**2**

Combine all 8 ingredients in small saucepan. Simmer, uncovered, over medium-low for 20 to 30 minutes, stirring frequently, until slightly thickened and onion is soft. Makes 2 cups (500 mL).

1 tbsp. (15 mL): 19 Calories; 0.2 g Total Fat; 133 mg Sodium; trace Protein; 4 g Carbohydrate; 1 g Dietary Fiber

Teriyaki Basting Sauce

Steak and chicken are delicious basted with this dark, sweet sauce.

Brown sugar, packed	1/3 **cup**	**75 mL**
Cornstarch	**2 tsp.**	**10 mL**
Ground ginger	**1 tsp.**	**5 mL**
Low-sodium soy sauce	1/2 **cup**	**125 mL**
Dry sherry (or alcohol-free sherry)	1/3 **cup**	**75 mL**
Lemon juice	**2 tbsp.**	**30 mL**
Garlic cloves, minced	**2**	**2**

Combine first 3 ingredients in small saucepan. ■ Stir in remaining 4 ingredients. Cook over medium-high until boiling and slightly thickened. Makes 1 scant cup (250 mL).

1 tbsp. (15 mL): 29 Calories; trace Total Fat; 315 mg Sodium; 1 g Protein; 6 g Carbohydrate; trace Dietary Fiber

Spicy Yogurt Marinade

Marinate beef, chicken or pork for the tenderizing enzyme action from the kiwifruit and also for the unusual but delicious flavors.

Plain low-fat yogurt	3/4 **cup**	**175 mL**
Peeled kiwifruit, cut into 4 chunks	**1**	**1**
Finely grated gingerroot	1/2 **tsp.**	**2 mL**
Garlic clove, minced	**1**	**1**
Ground cumin	1/2 **tsp.**	**2 mL**
Ground allspice	1/4 **tsp.**	**1 mL**
Ground cinnamon	1/4 **tsp.**	**1 mL**
Cayenne pepper	1/4 **tsp.**	**1 mL**
Salt	1/2 **tsp.**	**2 mL**

Process all 9 ingredients in blender. Makes 1 cup (250 mL).

1 tbsp. (15 mL): 11 Calories; 0.2 g Total Fat; 90 mg Sodium; 1 g Protein; 2 g Carbohydrate; trace Dietary Fiber

Black Currant Sauce

This flavorful sauce has a rich burgundy color. Once it is reduced, the thickness is just right for coating chicken or ribs.

Finely chopped red onion	**1 cup**	**250 mL**
Tub margarine	**1 tbsp.**	**15 mL**
Liquid honey	**1 tbsp.**	**15 mL**
Dry red (or alcohol-free red) wine	**¹/₂ cup**	**125 mL**
Red wine vinegar	**¹/₃ cup**	**75 mL**
Black currant jelly	**¹/₂ cup**	**125 mL**

Sauté red onion in margarine in large non-stick frying pan for about 15 minutes until red onion is soft and caramelized. ■ Stir in honey, wine and wine vinegar. Simmer for 2 minutes. ■ Stir in jelly until melted. Simmer for 18 minutes until thickened and reduced. Makes 1 cup (250 mL).

1 tbsp. (15 mL): 46 Calories; 0.7 g Total Fat; 12 mg Sodium; trace Protein; 9 g Carbohydrate; trace Dietary Fiber

Spicy Tomato Basting Sauce

Tangy with lots of spicy flavor. A real "BBQ" red. Try this on ribs or pork chops.

Tomato sauce	**7¹/₂ oz.**	**213 mL**
Finely chopped onion	**¹/₂ cup**	**125 mL**
Garlic clove, minced	**1**	**1**
White vinegar	**¹/₄ cup**	**60 mL**
Prepared mustard	**2 tbsp.**	**30 mL**
Chili powder	**1¹/₂ tsp.**	**7 mL**
Dried crushed chilies	**¹/₈ tsp.**	**0.5 mL**
Liquid honey	**¹/₄ cup**	**60 mL**

Combine first 7 ingredients in small saucepan. Bring to a boil. Reduce heat. Simmer, uncovered, over medium-low for 10 minutes. ■ Stir in honey. Makes 1¹/₃ cups (325 mL).

1 tbsp. (15 mL): 19 Calories; 0.1 g Total Fat; 81 mg Sodium; trace Protein; 5 g Carbohydrate; trace Dietary Fiber

Fiery Garlic Sauce

A very dark brown sauce with lots of "fire!"

Water	¹/₂ **cup**	**125 mL**
Cornstarch	**2 tsp.**	**10 mL**
Granulated sugar	**2 tbsp.**	**30 mL**
Apple cider vinegar	**2 tbsp.**	**30 mL**
Lemon juice	**2 tbsp.**	**30 mL**
Low-sodium soy sauce	**2 tbsp.**	**30 mL**
Dried crushed chilies	¹/₂ **tsp.**	**2 mL**
Garlic cloves, minced	**3**	**3**

Combine all 8 ingredients in small saucepan. Cook over medium, stirring constantly, until boiling and slightly thickened. Makes ³/₄ cup (175 mL).

1 tbsp. (15 mL): 13 Calories; trace Total Fat; 102 mg Sodium; trace Protein; 3 g Carbohydrate; trace Dietary Fiber

....

Don't have time on busy workdays to defrost the meat, mix the marinade and have the meat marinating for at least 2 to 4 hours? Purchase fresh (not previously frozen) boneless chicken breasts, less tender steaks and pork ribs in bulk. Make a large batch of your favorite marinade and have a supply of freezer bags on hand. Label the bags with the type of meat, quantity, and name of marinade (otherwise it might be hard to identify it). Divide the meat into enough servings for one meal and place in freezer bags. Carefully pour marinade into bags. Seal bags tightly, squeezing out all the air. Place bags in freezer. Meat will marinate during the freezing as well as the thawing process. On the day of serving, just take the bag out of the freezer in the morning and —voilà— ready-to-grill meat when you get home later in the day.

Hot 'N' Spicy Baste

Use for brushing on chicken. Enhancing the flavors of commercial barbecue sauce makes this a very easy sauce to prepare.

Commercial barbecue sauce	**$^1/_3$ cup**	**75 mL**
Chili sauce	**$^1/_3$ cup**	**75 mL**
Worcestershire sauce	**2 tsp.**	**10 mL**
Onion powder	**$^1/_4$ tsp.**	**1 mL**
Hot pepper sauce	**$^1/_4$ tsp.**	**1 mL**
Cayenne pepper, sprinkle		

Combine all 6 ingredients in small bowl. Stir to blend. Makes $^2/_3$ cup (150 mL).

1 tbsp. (15 mL): 16 Calories; 0.2 g Total Fat; 190 mg Sodium; trace Protein; 3 g Carbohydrate; 1 g Dietary Fiber

Dark Oriental Baste

Makes a shiny glaze that coats and darkens nicely. Enough for 8 to 10 pieces of chicken.

Seasoned salt	**1 tsp.**	**5 mL**
Dark soy sauce	**$^1/_3$ cup**	**75 ml**
Cooking molasses	**$^1/_4$ cup**	**60 mL**
Sesame oil	**2 tsp.**	**10 mL**
Ground ginger	**1 tsp.**	**5 mL**
Garlic powder	**$^1/_2$ tsp.**	**2 mL**

Combine all 6 ingredients in small bowl. Stir well. Makes about $^2/_3$ cup (150 mL).

1 tbsp. (15 mL): 33 Calories; 0.8 g Total Fat; 644 mg Sodium; 1 g Protein; 6 g Carbohydrate; trace Dietary Fiber

Pork & Lamb

here's nothing quicker or more delicious than ham steak cooked on a grill and basted with sauce until it's glazed. Both pork and lamb adapt well to the flavors of different herbs and spices. Pork tenderloin is particularly succulent when grilled and of course, what would barbecue season be without ribs!

Rosemary Lamb Chops

Rosemary and garlic complement the lamb nicely. There is also a hint of the balsamic if you go looking for it! Pictured on page 18.

Olive oil	$^1/_4$ **cup**	**60 mL**
Balsamic vinegar	2 tsp.	10 mL
Garlic cloves, minced	4	4
Chopped fresh rosemary leaves (or $^1/_2$ tsp., 2 mL, dried, crushed)	1 tbsp.	15 mL
Chopped fresh thyme leaves (or $^1/_4$ tsp., 1 mL, dried, crushed)	2 tsp.	10 mL
Small lean lamb chops, bone in ($^3/_4$-1 inch, 2-2.5 cm, thick)	1$^1/_2$ lbs.	680 g
Salt	$^1/_4$ tsp.	1 mL
Freshly ground pepper	$^1/_4$ tsp.	1 mL

Combine olive oil, vinegar, garlic, rosemary and thyme in small bowl. Makes $^1/_3$ cup (75 mL) marinade. ■ Spoon marinade over each side of chops in shallow casserole. Marinate at room temperature for 30 minutes. ■ Preheat lightly sprayed electric grill to high. Remove chops, reserving marinade. Sprinkle both sides of chops with salt and pepper. Sear on grill for 1 minute per side. Reduce heat to medium. Cook chops for 4 to 5 minutes per side, basting with reserved marinade several times, until desired doneness. Do not overcook. Best if left at medium doneness. Discard remaining marinade. Makes 8 small chops. Serves 4.

1 serving: 261 Calories; 19.4 g Total Fat; 225 mg Sodium; 20 g Protein; 1 g Carbohydrate; trace Dietary Fiber

Glazed Ham Steaks

Minutes to prepare after marinating. You'll love the golden glaze.

Apricot jam	$^1/_3$ **cup**	**75 mL**
Ginger ale	**3 tbsp.**	**50 mL**
French dressing	**3 tbsp.**	**50 mL**
Ground cumin	$^1/_2$ **tsp.**	**2 mL**
Ham steaks ($^1/_2$ inch, 12 mm, thick, about $^1/_2$ lb., 225 g, each)	**2**	**2**

Combine first 4 ingredients in small bowl. Heat in microwave on medium (50%), or in saucepan over medium, for about 1 minute. Makes $^3/_4$ cup (175 mL) marinade. ■ Pour over ham steak in shallow casserole. Marinate at room temperature for 1 hour, or covered in refrigerator for up to 24 hours. Preheat lightly sprayed electric grill to high. Remove steaks, reserving marinade. Cook ham steaks on grill for 4 to 5 minutes per side, basting with reserved marinade, until heated through and glazed. Discard any remaining marinade. Serves 4.

1 serving: 236 Calories; 8.5 g Total Fat; 1587 mg Sodium; 22 g Protein; 17 g Carbohydrate; trace Dietary Fiber

Pork Roast With Seasoned Crust

This is one of the best barbecued roasts—tender and moist with a crispy crust. Do not lift the lid except when turning the roast; you will lose valuable heat every time you do.

Garlic cloves, minced	**4**	**4**
Olive oil	**1 tbsp.**	**15 mL**
Paprika	**1 tsp.**	**5 mL**
Freshly ground pepper	**1 tsp.**	**5 mL**
Seasoned salt	**1 tsp.**	**5 mL**
Onion powder	$^1/_2$ **tsp.**	**2 mL**
Boneless pork leg (or shoulder butt) roast	**2$^1/_2$-3 lbs.**	**1.1-1.4 kg**

Combine garlic, olive oil and spices in small bowl to make a paste. Coat roast with seasoning mixture. Preheat barbecue to high. Place roast on greased grill over drip pan. Close lid. Cook, using indirect cooking method (see page 7), for 30 minutes. Turn roast. Reduce heat to medium. Close lid. Cook for 70 minutes, checking internal temperature with meat thermometer at 40 minutes. Final temperature should be 160°F (75°C). Serves 8.

1 serving: 395 Calories; 24.3 g Total Fat; 257 mg Sodium; 40 g Protein; 1 g Carbohydrate; trace Dietary Fiber

Chops with Ginger Orange Sauce

A hint of orange liqueur in the sauce makes these extra special.

Reserved mandarin orange juice (about $^1/_2$ **cup, 125 mL)**		
Low-sodium soy sauce	1 tbsp.	15 mL
Garlic clove, crushed	1	1
Finely grated gingerroot	$^1/_4$ tsp.	1 mL
Ground nutmeg	$^1/_{16}$ tsp.	0.5 mL
Pork loin chops ($^1/_2$ inch, 12 mm, thick)	4	4
Cornstarch	2 tsp.	10 mL
Canned mandarin orange segments, drained and juice reserved	10 oz.	284 mL
Orange-flavored liqueur (such as Triple Sec or Grand Marnier)	1 tbsp.	15 mL

Combine first 5 ingredients in small bowl. ■ Place pork chops in single layer in shallow casserole. Pour marinade over chops. Cover. Marinate in refrigerator for at least 4 hours or overnight, turning several times. ■ Preheat barbecue to medium. Drain and reserve marinade. Place chops on greased grill. Close lid. Cook for 10 minutes per side until desired doneness. Strain marinade into small saucepan. Combine 2 tbsp. (30 mL) marinade and cornstarch in small cup. Add to saucepan. Boil until slightly thickened. Stir in reserved orange segments and liqueur. Pour over pork chops. Serves 4.

1 serving: 312 Calories; 17.9 g Total Fat; 218 mg Sodium; 24 g Protein; 11 g Carbohydrate; trace Dietary Fiber

Chorizo And Rotini Dinner

This dinner is served warm with a pleasant heat coming from the sausage. Pictured on page 71.

Spicy chorizo sausages	**¹/₂ lb.**	**225 g**
Medium green pepper, quartered and seeded	**1**	**1**
Medium onion, peeled, root end intact, cut into 6 wedges	**1**	**1**
Garlic cloves, minced	**2**	**2**
Olive oil	**1¹/₂ tsp.**	**7 mL**
Fresh sweet basil leaves, stacked, rolled tightly lengthwise, then cut crosswise into very thin slivers (chiffonade)	**10**	**10**
Medium tomato, diced	**1**	**1**
Rotini pasta (about 2¹/₄ cups, 560 mL)	**6 oz.**	**170 g**
Boiling water	**2¹/₂ qts.**	**2.5 L**
Salt	**1 tbsp.**	**15 mL**
Grated Parmesan cheese (optional)	**2 tbsp.**	**30 mL**

Preheat lightly sprayed electric grill to medium-high. Poke sausages with fork in several places. Place sausages, green pepper quarters and onion wedges on grill. Cook for about 5 minutes, turning sausages and vegetables several times, until sausages are cooked. Cut into thin slices. Dice cooked vegetables. ■ Lightly sauté garlic in olive oil in small non-stick skillet for a few seconds. Stir in basil and diced tomato just until fragrant and warmed. Remove from heat. ■ Cook pasta in boiling water and salt in large uncovered pot or Dutch oven for 7 to 9 minutes, stirring occasionally, until tender. Drain. Put into large bowl. ■ Pour tomato mixture over pasta. Add sausage and vegetables. Toss together. Sprinkle with Parmesan cheese. Toss. Makes about 7 cups (1.75 L). Serves 4.

1 serving: 393 Calories; 20.2 g Total Fat; 419 mg Sodium; 14 g Protein; 38 g Carbohydrate; 2 g Dietary Fiber

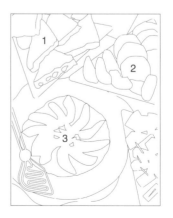

1. Fruity Streusel Toast, page 135
2. Margaritagrill, page 74
3. Apple And Cheese Pizza, page 77

Raspberry Tenderloin

Cracked peppercorns give an explosion of flavor and seem to blend so well with the raspberry. A unique way to enjoy pork.

Pork tenderloin	**1 lb.**	**454 g**
Whole black peppercorns, cracked in plastic bag with mallet	**1 tsp.**	**5 mL**
Reserved raspberry syrup		
Apple cider vinegar	**1 tbsp.**	**15 mL**
Hoisin sauce	**1 tsp.**	**5 mL**
Liquid honey	**1 tbsp.**	**15 mL**
Cornstarch	**1 tsp.**	**5 mL**
Frozen raspberries in syrup, drained and syrup reserved	**15 oz.**	**425 g**

Preheat barbecue to medium-high. Cut pork tenderloin lengthwise in half but not quite through to other side. Open tenderloin along cut and press to flatten evenly. Sprinkle with pepper on both sides. ■ Combine reserved raspberry syrup and vinegar in small saucepan. Carefully dab vinegar mixture over top surface of tenderloin. ■ Add hoisin sauce, honey and cornstarch to remaining liquid in saucepan. Boil hard for about 5 minutes until slightly reduced. Makes ³/₄ cup (175 mL) basting sauce. Place pork on greased grill. Close lid. Cook for 3 minutes. Turn, basting cooked surface with sauce. Cook for 3 minutes. Turn and baste with sauce. Cook for about 4 minutes, turning and basting several more times, watching carefully so as not to burn, until desired doneness. ■ Reheat remaining sauce to boiling. Cool. Stir in reserved raspberries. Slice pork into ¹/₄ inch (6 mm) thick slices. Serve with warm sauce over top or on the side. Serves 4.

1 serving: 221 Calories; 2.8 g Total Fat; 126 mg Sodium; 16 g Protein; 34 g Carbohydrate; 5 g Dietary Fiber

1. Bulgur Patties, page 47
2. Vegetarian Chili On A Bun, page 131
3. Stuffed Peppers, page 149

Stuffed Tenderloin

A little bit of an apple and bread stuffing in every bite. Pictured on page 53.

Pork tenderloins (about $^1/_2$ lb., 225 g, each) Freshly ground pepper, sprinkle	2	2
Canola oil	1 tsp.	5 mL
Finely chopped onion	$^1/_4$ cup	60 mL
Small garlic clove, minced	1	1
Small red apple, with peel, finely chopped	1	1
Chopped fresh thyme leaves (or $^1/_8$-$^1/_4$ tsp., 0.5-1 mL, dried)	$^1/_2$-1 tsp.	2-5 mL
Fresh bread crumbs (about 1 slice bread, with crusts, processed in blender)	$^3/_4$ cup	175 mL
Salt	$^1/_8$ tsp.	0.5 mL
Freshly ground pepper	$^1/_8$ tsp.	0.5 mL
Canola oil	1 tbsp.	15 mL
Apple cider vinegar	1 tbsp.	15 mL
Chopped fresh thyme leaves (or $^1/_8$-$^1/_4$ tsp., 0.5-1 mL, dried)	$^1/_2$-1 tsp.	2-5 mL

Preheat barbecue to medium-high. Cut tenderloins lengthwise in half but not quite through to other side. Open tenderloin along cut and press to flatten evenly. Sprinkle cut surface with pepper. ■ Heat first amount of oil in medium non-stick skillet. Sauté onion and garlic for about 2 minutes until onion is slightly soft. ■ Stir in apple. Sauté for 2 to 3 minutes until apple is slightly soft. ■ Stir in first amount of thyme, bread crumbs, salt and pepper. Makes 1 cup (250 mL) stuffing. Pack $^1/_2$ cup (125 mL) stuffing lengthwise down middle, on cut side, of each tenderloin. Roll to enclose filling. Tie with butcher's string or skewer together. ■ Combine remaining 3 ingredients in small bowl. Place tenderloins on greased grill. Close lid. Cook for 10 to 15 minutes, turning several times and basting with oil mixture, until desired doneness. Cut into about ten, $^1/_2$ inch (12 mm) thick slices. Serves 4.

1 serving: 240 Calories; 8.3 g Total Fat; 311 mg Sodium; 18 g Protein; 23 g Carbohydrate; 1 g Dietary Fiber

Spicy Chops

Very tender chops with just a hint of curry coming through.

Juice (about ¹/₄ cup, 60 mL) and finely grated peel of 1 medium lemon		
Low-sodium soy sauce	1 tbsp.	15 mL
Garlic cloves, minced	2	2
Curry paste	1 tsp.	5 mL
Ground coriander	1 tsp.	5 mL
Seasoned salt	¹/₂ tsp.	2 mL
Cayenne pepper	¹/₈ tsp.	0.5 mL
Small boneless pork loin chops (about 1 lb., 454 g)	4	4

Combine first 7 ingredients in small bowl. Makes about ¹/₄ cup (60 mL) marinade.
■ Place pork chops in shallow glass dish or casserole. Pour marinade over. Marinate in refrigerator for several hours or overnight. Drain and discard marinade. Preheat lightly sprayed electric grill to medium. Cook pork chops on grill for 10 to 15 minutes, turning frequently, until no pink remains. Serves 4.

1 serving: 141 Calories; 3.2 g Total Fat; 359 mg Sodium; 25 g Protein; 4 g Carbohydrate; 1 g Dietary Fiber

ORANGE GLAZED SPICY CHOPS: Combine ¹/₄ cup (60 mL) marmalade and 2 tbsp. (30 mL) hot water in small bowl. Baste each side of pork chops with diluted marmalade for last 2 to 3 minutes of cooking.

....

Don't turn meat with a fork, or cut into it with a knife to test for doneness during cooking. Piercing the sealed surface will let valuable juices escape, resulting in tougher, drier meat. Instead, use tongs to turn or to squeeze meat for firmness. A gentle squeeze will also release some juices for a visual test (see Tip, page 29).

Honey Garlic Ribs

These are so finger-licking good, they'll soon be a favorite! Precooking eliminates a lot of excess fat and tenderizes the ribs before glazing.

Pork side ribs, trimmed and cut into about 6-rib sections	3 lbs.	1.4 kg
Boiling water	12 cups	3 L
Bay leaf	1	1
Freshly ground pepper, sprinkle		
Liquid honey	$^1/_3$ cup	75 mL
Lemon juice	$^1/_3$ cup	75 mL
Low-sodium soy sauce	3 tbsp.	50 mL
Garlic cloves, minced	3	3
Sherry (or alcohol-free sherry)	$1^1/_2$ tbsp.	25 mL

Cook ribs in boiling water, bay leaf and pepper in large pot or Dutch oven for about 45 minutes until almost tender. Discard liquid and bay leaf, or strain and use for soup. ■ Combine remaining 5 ingredients in small bowl. Makes $^3/_4$ cup (175 mL) basting sauce. Preheat lightly sprayed electric grill to medium. Cook ribs on grill for 10 to 15 minutes, turning and basting several times, until glazed and golden. Discard any remaining sauce. Serves 4.

1 serving: 407 Calories; 15.4 g Total Fat; 564 mg Sodium; 41 g Protein; 25 g Carbohydrate; trace Dietary Fiber

Country-Style Ribs

Only baste these with glaze during the last ten minutes of cooking to prevent burning.

Country-style pork ribs	3 lbs.	1.4 kg
Freshly ground pepper, sprinkle		
Apple juice	$^1/_3$ cup	75 mL
Maple (or maple-flavored) syrup	$^1/_3$ cup	75 mL
Garlic powder	$^3/_4$ tsp.	4 mL
Onion powder	$^3/_4$ tsp.	4 mL
Dried crushed chilies	$^1/_2$ tsp.	2 mL

(continued on next page)

Preheat lightly sprayed electric grill to medium. Sprinkle ribs with pepper. Cook on grill for about 40 minutes, turning several times, until almost cooked. ■ Combine remaining 5 ingredients in small bowl. Makes ²/₃ cup (150 mL) basting sauce. Brush ribs with sauce. Cook for about 10 minutes, turning and basting, until glazed and browned. Discard any remaining sauce. Serves 4.

1 serving: 382 Calories; 15.5 g Total Fat; 140 mg Sodium; 40 g Protein; 19 g Carbohydrate; trace Dietary Fiber

Canadian Maple Ribs

Real Canadian maple syrup will give the best flavor.

Maple (or maple-flavored) syrup	**²/₃ cup**	**150 mL**
Brown sugar, packed	**2 tbsp.**	**30 mL**
Ketchup	**2 tbsp.**	**30 mL**
Apple cider vinegar	**4 tsp.**	**20 mL**
Worcestershire sauce	**4 tsp.**	**20 mL**
Prepared mustard	**4 tsp.**	**20 mL**
Salt	**1 tsp.**	**5 mL**
Baby back ribs (about 2 racks)	**2¹/₂ lbs.**	**1.1 kg**

Preheat barbecue to high. Whisk first 7 ingredients together in small bowl. Makes 1 cup (250 mL) sauce. ■ Place racks of ribs on greased grill. Brush with sauce. Cook for 2 minutes to sear. Turn over. Brush with sauce. Cook for 2 minutes to sear. Reduce temperature to medium. Close lid. Cook for 30 to 40 minutes, turning and basting several times, until ribs are glazed and tender. Discard any remaining sauce. Serves 4.

1 serving: 490 Calories; 17.8 g Total Fat; 887 mg Sodium; 37 g Protein; 45 g Carbohydrate; trace Dietary Fiber

Salads

es you can grill a salad … or at least some of the ingredients in it! These recipes may look lengthy, but they are so unique and delicious that you will find the extra effort well worth the time. These recipes are hearty salads that just need a basket of buns and a light dessert to complete the meal.

Herbed Polenta And Chicken Salad

Impress your company with this very showy salad. Wonderful mix of flavors! Pictured on front cover.

Boneless, skinless chicken breast halves (about 4)	1 lb.	454 g
Non-fat (or low-fat) Italian dressing	1/2 cup	125 mL
Condensed chicken broth	2 × 10 oz.	2 × 284 mL
Water	1 1/4 cups	300 mL
Yellow cornmeal	1 cup	250 mL
Tub margarine	1 tbsp.	15 mL
Salt	1/2 tsp.	2 mL
Snipped fresh chives (or 2 tsp., 10 mL, dried)	2 tbsp.	30 mL
Finely chopped fresh marjoram leaves (or 1 tsp., 5 mL, dried)	1 tbsp.	15 mL
Freshly ground pepper, sprinkle		
Olive oil	1 tbsp.	15 mL
Torn mixed dark salad greens, lightly packed (such as spinach and romaine)	6 cups	1.5 L
Medium tomatoes, cut into 8 wedges each	2	2
Large carrot, peeled into ribbons	1	1
Non-fat (or low-fat) Italian dressing	2/3 cup	150 mL
Grated Parmesan cheese (optional)	1/4 cup	60 mL
Freshly ground pepper, sprinkle		

(continued on next page)

Cut 3 deep gashes in top of each chicken breast half. Place in shallow glass dish or casserole. Pour first amount of dressing over chicken. Marinate at room temperature for 20 minutes. Chicken can be covered and marinated in refrigerator for longer if desired. Preheat lightly sprayed electric grill to medium. Remove chicken and reserve dressing for basting. Cook chicken on grill for 20 to 25 minutes, turning and basting several times, until no pink remains. Remove to plate. Discard any remaining dressing. Cover chicken with foil to keep warm. ■ Bring broth and water to a boil in large saucepan. Reduce heat. Slowly add cornmeal, 1 tbsp. (15 mL) at a time, stirring constantly while liquid gently boils. Stir and cook for about 15 minutes until polenta pulls away from sides of saucepan and is very thick. ■ Stir in margarine, salt, chives, marjoram and pepper. Pack polenta evenly into 9 x 13 inch (22 x 33 cm) pan that has been greased with 1¹/₂ tsp. (7 mL) olive oil. Brush remaining olive oil over surface of polenta. Cool. Turn firm polenta out onto cutting board. Cut into 4 equal lengthwise strips. Cut again, on the diagonal to make diamond shapes. Cook polenta on grill for about 2 minutes per side until warmed through and crispy. ■ Arrange bed of lettuce on each of 4 plates. Surround lettuce with tomato wedges and carrot ribbons. Thinly slice chicken on diagonal and arrange over lettuce in fanned shape. Add 2 pieces polenta to each plate. Serve remaining pieces on the side. ■ Immediately before serving, drizzle each serving with about 2 tbsp. (30 mL) dressing. Sprinkle each with 1 tbsp. (15 mL) cheese and pepper. Serves 4.

1 serving (with 2 wedges Polenta): 247 Calories; 4 g Total Fat; 1167 mg Sodium; 32 g Protein; 20 g Carbohydrate; 3 g Dietary Fiber

. . . .

To prevent your indoor grill from smoking, trim excess fat from meats and don't use sugar-based marinades—save them for your outdoor barbecuing.

Grilled Vegetable And Bread Salad

If you like feta cheese and balsamic vinegar, you are going to love this salad.

Olive oil	$^1/_3$ cup	75 mL
Garlic cloves, minced	2	2
Medium zucchini, with peel, sliced lengthwise into 4 slices	1	1
Medium red pepper, quartered and seeded	1	1
Medium yellow or orange pepper, quartered and seeded	1	1
Medium red onion, sliced into thick slices	1	1
Medium roma (plum) tomatoes, halved	4	4
Salt, sprinkle		
Freshly ground pepper, sprinkle		
Multi-grain or whole wheat bread, cut into 1 inch (2.5 cm) slices (about 5)	4 cups	1 L
Non-fat Italian dressing	$^1/_3$ cup	75 mL
Balsamic vinegar	$^1/_4$ cup	60 mL
Basil pesto	3 tbsp.	50 mL
Coarsely chopped ripe olives, drained	$^1/_4$ cup	60 mL
Feta cheese, crumbled (about $^2/_3$ cup, 150 mL), optional	4 oz.	113 g

Preheat lightly sprayed electric grill to medium. Combine olive oil and garlic in small bowl. ■ Brush vegetables with garlic oil. Cook on grill for 5 to 12 minutes depending on vegetable. Tomatoes require least amount of time so keep them to outer edge. Brush vegetables with more oil as needed while turning several times. Sprinkle with salt and pepper to taste. Remove vegetables to cutting board as they become soft. Dice vegetables and place in large bowl. ■ Brush remaining garlic oil over each side of bread slice. Toast on grill until golden. Cube into 1 inch (2.5 cm) pieces and reserve. ■ Combine dressing, vinegar, pesto and chopped olives in small bowl. Pour over diced vegetables. Toss to combine. Let stand for 15 minutes for flavors to meld (or cover and marinate in refrigerator for up to 8 hours). Just before serving, bring to room temperature and toss with reserved bread cubes and cheese. Makes 8 cups (2 L), enough for 6 servings.

1 serving: 241 Calories; 16.6 g Total Fat; 343 mg Sodium; 4 g Protein; 23 g Carbohydrate; 4 g Dietary Fiber

Jamaican Chicken Salad

A nice sweet salad with a nippy finish. You don't have to travel to Jamaica to relish these flavors.

Brown sugar, packed	2 tsp.	10 mL
Dried thyme, crushed	1 tsp.	5 mL
Ground allspice	1/2 tsp.	2 mL
Cayenne pepper	1/4-1/2 tsp.	1-2 mL
Salt	1/4 tsp.	1 mL
Ground nutmeg	1/4 tsp.	1 mL
Freshly ground pepper, generous sprinkle		
Ground cloves, light sprinkle		
Boneless, skinless chicken breast halves (about 3/4 lb., 340 g)	3	3
Canola oil	3 tbsp.	50 mL
Firm, slightly green banana, peeled and halved lengthwise	1	1
Canned pineapple slices, drained and juice reserved	19 oz.	540 mL
Medium red pepper, quartered and seeded	1	1
Freshly squeezed lime juice	2 tbsp.	30 mL
Liquid honey	1/4 cup	60 mL
Reserved pineapple juice	1/4 cup	60 mL
Ripe medium avocado, peeled and diced	1	1
Shredded lettuce, lightly packed	6 cups	1.5 L

Combine first 8 ingredients in small bowl. Makes 5 tsp. (25 mL) coating. ■ Pound chicken breasts to even thickness. Sprinkle both sides with 1 tbsp. (15 mL) brown sugar mixture, reserving remainder. Let chicken breasts stand at room temperature for about 10 minutes. ■ Stir reserved seasoning with oil. Brush banana, pineapple slices and red peppers with oil. Preheat barbecue to medium. Place fruit and vegetables on greased grill. Close lid. Cook for 5 to 15 minutes (depending on fruit or vegetable), turning several times, until soft. Cut banana into chunks, pineapple into quarters and red pepper into slivers and place in large bowl. Cook chicken on grill for 20 to 25 minutes until no longer pink. Remove and cut into slivers. Add to large bowl. Toss. ■ Combine lime juice, honey and reserved pineapple juice in small bowl. Add avocado. Toss to coat. Pour all over chicken mixture in large bowl. Divide lettuce among 4 salad plates. Immediately spoon warm chicken mixture over lettuce. Serves 4.

1 serving: 482 Calories; 19.8 g Total Fat; 245 mg Sodium; 24 g Protein; 58 g Carbohydrate; 5 g Dietary Fiber

Warm Pesto Salad

This salad takes a little more time, but is well worth the effort. Can be served as a main course.

Olive oil	1/2 cup	125 mL
Large garlic cloves, coarsely chopped	5	5
Coarsely chopped fresh sweet basil leaves	1/2 cup	125 mL
Chopped fresh parsley	1/4 cup	60 mL
Freshly ground pepper, sprinkle		
Medium Japanese eggplant, cut into lengthwise slices about 1/4 inch (6 mm) thick	1	1
Cob of corn, husked	1	1
Small red (or Spanish) onion, cut into thick slices	1	1
Small yellow pepper, halved and seeded	1	1
Small red pepper, halved and seeded	1	1
Large head radicchio, quartered	1	1
Top sirloin steak (1 inch, 2.5 cm, thick), trimmed of fat	3/4 lb.	340 g
Mixed greens, torn bite size	6 cups	1.5 L
Roma (plum) tomatoes, diced	2	2
Grated Parmesan cheese	2 tbsp.	30 mL

Preheat barbecue to high. Process first 5 ingredients in blender, scraping down sides as needed until smooth. Makes 2/3 cup (150 mL) basting sauce. ■ Brush sauce heavily on eggplant slices. ■ Brush sauce lightly on corn, red onion, peppers, radicchio and steak, using up all of sauce. Sear steak on greased grill for 1 minute per side. Cook for 3 to 4 minutes per side until desired doneness. Reduce heat to medium. Remove steak to cutting board. Place vegetables on greased grill. Close lid. Cook for about 10 minutes, turning occasionally, until tender-crisp and corn kernels are starting to pop. As they are cooked, remove to cutting board and dice into bite-size pieces. Cut corn off cob. Place all vegetables in large bowl. Slice steak very thinly across grain. Add to vegetables. ■ Add mixed greens. Toss together well. Add tomato and cheese. Serve immediately. Makes about 12 cups (3 L) with lettuce and tomato. Serves 6.

1 serving: 326 Calories; 22.6 g Total Fat; 96 mg Sodium; 16 g Protein; 18 g Carbohydrate; 5 g Dietary Fiber

Skewers

presentation at mealtime can be so interesting and attractive when food is grilled and served on skewers. Use your creative eye when you assemble the food on each skewer. Keep in mind color, size, and overall "design." The type and shape of skewer itself will also determine to some degree what the finished look will be. There are a number of kinds of skewers available (see Skewers, page 8). Look for unique handles and shapes too. The recipes in this section work best on flat-sided and two-pronged skewers because the food can't "spin around" as the skewer is turned. But all designs work reasonably well.

Kiwi-Marinated Beef

Don't be surprised by the name. The kiwi does a great job of tenderizing the beef.

Low-sodium soy sauce	**¹/₄ cup**	**60 mL**
Water	**¹/₄ cup**	**60 mL**
Green onion, cut into 4 pieces	**1**	**1**
Garlic cloves, peeled	**2**	**2**
Kiwifruit, peeled and cut into 4 chunks	**1**	**1**
Finely grated gingerroot	**1 tsp.**	**5 mL**
Brown sugar, packed	**1 tbsp.**	**15 mL**
Sesame seeds	**2 tbsp.**	**30 mL**
Dried crushed chilies	**¹/₂ tsp.**	**2 mL**
Top sirloin steak (1 inch, 2.5 cm, thick), trimmed of fat	**1¹/₂ lbs.**	**680 g**
10 inch (25 cm) bamboo skewers, soaked in water for 10 minutes	**6**	**6**

Combine first 9 ingredients in blender. Process until no large chunks remain. Makes 1 cup (250 mL) marinade. ■ Cut steak into long ¹/₄ inch (6 mm) wide strips across grain. Place in large sealable plastic bag. Pour in marinade. Seal bag. Mix marinade into beef by turning bag several times. Marinate in refrigerator for no longer than 2 hours, mixing contents several times. (If beef is left too long in the marinade it will start to break down and become mushy.) Preheat lightly sprayed electric grill to high. Drain and discard marinade. Push beef onto skewers, accordion style. Cook on grill for 3 to 5 minutes, turning several times, until desired doneness. Makes 6 skewers.

1 skewer: 166 Calories; 5.3 g Total Fat; 380 mg Sodium; 24 g Protein; 5 g Carbohydrate; 1 g Dietary Fiber

Spicy Threaded Beef

A nice heat from the chilies with a zip from the lime.

Flank steak	1^1/$_2$ lbs.	680 g
Low-sodium soy sauce	^{1}/$_4$ cup	60 mL
Tequila	^{1}/$_4$ cup	60 mL
Freshly squeezed juice of 2 limes		
Small hot chilies, seeds removed and chopped fine (see Note)	3	3
Garlic cloves, minced	4	4
Finely grated gingerroot	1 tbsp.	15 mL
Canola oil	1 tbsp.	15 mL
10 inch (25 cm) bamboo skewers, soaked in water for 10 minutes	12	12
Prepared orange juice	^{1}/$_2$ cup	125 mL
Brown sugar, packed	1 tbsp.	15 mL
Cornstarch	2 tsp.	10 mL

Cut steak on diagonal across grain into ^{1}/$_2$ inch (12 mm) thick slices. (This is easier to do if steak is partially frozen.) Place in sealable plastic bag. ■ Combine next 7 ingredients in small bowl. Makes ^{2}/$_3$ cup (150 mL) marinade. Pour over beef strips. Seal bag. Marinate in refrigerator for several hours or overnight, turning several times. ■ Drain and reserve marinade. Push beef strips onto skewers, accordion style. ■ Strain remaining marinade through sieve. Discard solids. Add orange juice to strained marinade in small saucepan. Combine brown sugar and cornstarch in small cup. Stir into mixture in saucepan. Bring to a boil, stirring until thickened. Makes ^{3}/$_4$ cup (175 mL) sauce. Preheat lightly sprayed electric grill to medium-high. Place skewers on grill. Cook for about 3 minutes per side, basting occasionally with thickened sauce, until desired doneness. Reheat remaining sauce to boiling before serving. Makes 12 skewers.

1 skewer: 115 Calories; 6.2 g Total Fat; 255 mg Sodium; 13 g Protein; 6 g Carbohydrate; trace Dietary Fiber

Note: When chopping hot peppers use gloves, as the caustic oily compounds, called capsaicin (kap-SAY-ih-sihn), permeate the skin and can cause a burning sensation.

Bourguignonne Skewers

Serve these with buttered noodles and any leftover sauce. Pictured on page 107.

RED WINE SAUCE		
Dry (or alcohol-free) red wine	**1 cup**	**250 mL**
Tomato juice	**1 cup**	**250 mL**
Condensed beef bouillon	**10 oz.**	**284 mL**
Worcestershire sauce	**4 tsp.**	**20 mL**
Garlic cloves, minced	**4**	**4**
Dried thyme	**1 tsp.**	**5 mL**
Freshly ground pepper	**$1/4$ tsp.**	**1 mL**
Bay leaves	**4**	**4**
Top sirloin steak, cut into 18, $1^1/2$ inch (3.8 cm) cubes, trimmed of fat	**1 lb.**	**454 g**
Medium carrots, cut into 18, $1/2$ inch (12 mm) chunks and partially cooked	**2**	**2**
Large onion, cut into 6 wedges	**1**	**1**
Cornstarch	**2 tbsp.**	**30 mL**
Medium fresh mushrooms	**18**	**18**
Long metal skewers	**6**	**6**

Red Wine Sauce: Combine first 8 ingredients in medium bowl. Makes $3^1/4$ cups (800 mL) marinade. ■ Add steak cubes, carrot chunks and onion wedges. Stir gently to coat well. Cover. Marinate in refrigerator for 4 hours or overnight. ■ Drain marinade into medium saucepan. Stir in cornstarch. Heat over medium. Boil until thickened. ■ Preheat barbecue to medium-high. Alternate 1 meat, 1 carrot, 1 onion, 1 mushroom, ending with 1 meat, on each skewer. Place skewers on greased grill. Close lid. Cook for 8 to 10 minutes, turning and basting frequently, until desired doneness. Reheat remaining sauce to boiling before serving. Makes 6 skewers.

1 skewer: 183 Calories; 3.3 g Total Fat; 552 mg Sodium; 19 g Protein; 13 g Carbohydrate; 2 g Dietary Fiber

Middle East Kibbe

Pronounced KIH-bee. A hint of mint and cumin in an exotic ground beef and bulgur morsel. Serve with Cool Yogurt Dip, page 14.

Bulgur wheat	6 tbsp.	100 mL
Hot water (not boiling)	1/2 cup	125 mL
Lean ground beef	3/4 lb.	340 g
Large egg	1	1
Finely chopped onion	2 tbsp.	30 mL
Lemon juice	1 1/2 tsp.	7 mL
Coarsely chopped toasted pine nuts	2 tbsp.	30 mL
Ground cumin	1/2 tsp.	2 mL
Salt	3/4 tsp.	4 mL
Ground coriander	1/2 tsp.	2 mL
Cayenne pepper	1/4 tsp.	1 mL
Chopped fresh mint leaves, not packed	2 tsp.	10 mL
Long flat-sided metal skewers	8	8

Preheat lightly sprayed electric grill to medium-high. Soak bulgur in hot water in small bowl for 15 minutes until soft. Drain. Squeeze dry. ■ Combine remaining 10 ingredients in medium bowl. Stir in bulgur. Divide into 16 equal portions. Form 2 portions individually, into cigar shapes around skewer. Repeat. ■ Place skewers on grill. Cook for about 10 minutes, turning several times, until beef is no longer pink. Makes 8 skewers.

1 skewer: 91 Calories; 4.3 g Total Fat; 278 mg Sodium; 8 g Protein; 6 g Carbohydrate; 2 g Dietary Fiber

Chicken Yakitori

Make these on small skewers if you want to use as appetizers.

Long metal skewers	8	8
Boneless, skinless chicken breast halves (about 1/2 lb., 225 g), cut into lengthwise strips	2	2
Green onions, cut into 1 1/2 inch (3.8 cm) pieces	2	2
Medium yellow pepper, seeded and cut into 1 1/2 inch (3.8 cm) pieces	1	1
Low-sodium soy sauce	1/4 cup	60 mL
Dry sherry (or alcohol-free sherry)	1/4 cup	60 mL
Liquid honey	2 tbsp.	30 mL
Garlic clove, minced	1	1

(continued on next page)

Push skewer through end of 1 chicken slice. Push on green onion. Push chicken strips, accordion style, back and forth over alternating green onion and yellow pepper pieces. Repeat for remaining skewers. ■ Combine soy sauce, sherry, honey and garlic in pie plate or shallow casserole. Makes $^1/_2$ cup (125 mL) marinade. Lay skewers in single layer in marinade. Turn over to coat. Cover. Marinate in refrigerator for several hours or overnight. Preheat barbecue to medium-low. Drain and discard marinade. Place skewers on greased grill. Close lid. Cook for about 15 minutes, turning several times, until chicken is cooked. Makes 8 skewers.

1 skewer: 60 Calories; 0.8 g Total Fat; 262 mg Sodium; 7 g Protein; 5 g Carbohydrate; trace Dietary Fiber

Tandoori Chicken Sticks

Normally these would be cooked in a tandoor oven in India, but the yogurt and seasonings still impart a lot of the traditional flavor. Serve these with Chili Peanut Sauce, page 21.

Plain low-fat yogurt	$^1/_2$ **cup**	**125 mL**
Lemon juice	**4 tsp.**	**20 mL**
Garlic cloves, minced	**2**	**2**
Finely grated gingerroot	**2 tsp.**	**10 mL**
Hot pepper sauce	$^1/_2$ **tsp.**	**2 mL**
Ground cumin	$^1/_2$ **tsp.**	**2 mL**
Paprika	$^1/_2$ **tsp.**	**2 mL**
Salt	$^1/_2$ **tsp.**	**2 mL**
Ground coriander	$^1/_4$ **tsp.**	**1 mL**
Boneless, skinless chicken breast halves (about 1 lb., 454 g)	**4**	**4**
6 inch (15 cm) bamboo skewers, soaked in water for 10 minutes	**8**	**8**

Combine first 9 ingredients in medium bowl. Makes $^2/_3$ cup (150 mL) marinade. ■ Cut chicken into bite-size pieces. Add to marinade. Stir to coat well. Cover. Marinate in refrigerator for several hours or overnight. ■ Preheat lightly sprayed electric grill to medium. Drain and discard marinade. Push chicken onto skewers. Place skewers on grill. Cook for 12 to 15 minutes, turning frequently, until chicken is cooked. Makes 8 skewers.

1 skewer: 82 Calories; 1.9 g Total Fat; 169 mg Sodium; 14 g Protein; 1 g Carbohydrate; trace Dietary Fiber

Apple Chicken Brochettes

Cinnamony, sweet sauce is reminiscent of valentine heart candy!

Boneless, skinless chicken breast halves (about $^1/_2$ lb., 225 g)	**2**	**2**
Long flat-sided metal skewers	**12**	**12**
Medium red apples, with peel, cored, cut into 6 wedges each and then halved crosswise	**2**	**2**
Large red onion, cut into 1-1$^1/_2$ inch (2.5-3.8 cm) dice	**1**	**1**
SPICY SAUCE		
Red currant jelly	$^1/_2$ **cup**	**125 mL**
Water	$^1/_4$ **cup**	**60 mL**
Chicken bouillon powder	$^1/_2$ **tsp.**	**2 mL**
Ground cinnamon	$^1/_4$ **tsp.**	**1 mL**
Ground allspice	$^1/_8$ **tsp.**	**0.5 mL**
Freshly ground pepper, sprinkle		

Slice chicken breasts lengthwise while slightly frozen into twelve $^1/_4$ inch (6 mm) thick slices. ■ Push skewer through end of 1 chicken slice. Push on 1 apple piece. Zig-zag chicken slice back and forth over alternating apple and red onion pieces. Repeat to make 12 skewers. ■ **Spicy Sauce:** Combine all 6 ingredients in small saucepan. Heat to boiling over medium. Makes $^1/_2$ cup (125 mL) basting sauce. Preheat barbecue to medium-high. Place skewers on greased grill. Close lid. Cook for 8 to 10 minutes, turning and basting with sauce several times, until chicken is no longer pink. Discard any remaining sauce. Makes 12 brochettes.

1 brochette: 75 Calories; 0.7 g Total Fat; 38 mg Sodium; 5 g Protein; 13 g Carbohydrate; 1 g Dietary Fiber

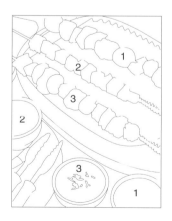

1. Lamb Kabobs (with Herb And Mint Sauce), page 121
2. Hawaiian Ham Skewers (with Sweet And Sour Sauce), page 109
3. Bourguignonne Skewers (with Red Wine Sauce), page 103

Hawaiian Ham Skewers

Only a hint of sweetness. Very attractive, with a glistening coat and dark grill lines. Pictured on page 107.

SWEET AND SOUR SAUCE		
Reserved pineapple juice	**$^1/_2$ cup**	**125 mL**
Low-sodium soy sauce	**$^1/_4$ cup**	**60 mL**
Liquid honey	**$^1/_4$ cup**	**60 mL**
Dijon mustard	**1 tbsp.**	**15 mL**
Finely grated gingerroot	**1-2 tsp.**	**5-10 mL**
Lean ham, cut into 1 inch (2.5 cm) cubes	**1 lb.**	**454 g**
Cornstarch	**2 tsp.**	**10 mL**
Canned pineapple chunks, drained and juice reserved	**14 oz.**	**398 mL**
Ripe large mango (or papaya), peeled and cut into cubes same size as pineapple chunks	**1**	**1**
Long metal skewers	**8**	**8**

Sweet And Sour Sauce: Combine pineapple juice, soy sauce, honey, mustard and ginger in medium bowl. Makes about 1 cup (250 mL) marinade. ■ Add ham. Cover. Marinate in refrigerator for several hours or overnight. Preheat lightly sprayed electric grill to medium-high. Drain and reserve marinade in small saucepan. ■ Mix cornstarch and 2 tbsp. (30 mL) marinade in small cup. Add to marinade in saucepan. Heat, stirring continually, until sauce is boiling and thickened. ■ Alternate pieces of pineapple, mango and ham on each skewer. Cook on grill for 8 to 10 minutes, turning and basting with sauce several times, until hot and glazed. Reheat remaining sauce to boiling before serving. Makes 8 skewers.

1 skewer: 167 Calories; 3.1 g Total Fat; 1168 mg Sodium; 12 g Protein; 24 g Carbohydrate; 1 g Dietary Fiber

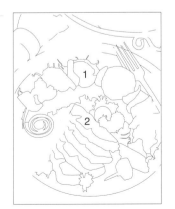

1. Curried Vegetables, page 119
2. Stuffed Steak, page 32

Sweet But Spicy Pork

Serve on a bed of rice with remaining sauce.

Large rutabaga, peeled and cut into 1¹/₂ inch (3.8 cm) cubes	¹/₂	¹/₂
Water	3 cups	750 mL
Medium fresh pineapple, peeled, cored and cut into 1¹/₂ inch (3.8 cm) cubes	1	1
Medium red onion, cut into 1¹/₂ inch (3.8 cm) chunks	1	1
Pork tenderloin, cut into 1¹/₂ inch (3.8 cm) cubes (about 20 chunks)	1 lb.	454 g
Long metal skewers	6	6
Finely chopped onion	¹/₂ cup	125 mL
Finely diced jalapeño pepper, ribs and seeds discarded (see Note)	1	1
Canola oil	2 tsp.	10 mL
Canned mango slices, drained and fruit puréed in blender	14 oz.	398 mL
Chopped mango chutney	¹/₄ cup	60 mL
Liquid honey	2 tbsp.	30 mL
Chili sauce	2 tbsp.	30 mL
Ground cumin	¹/₄ tsp.	1 mL
Ground coriander	¹/₈ tsp.	0.5 mL

Boil rutabaga cubes in water in large saucepan until tender but firm when poked with tip of knife. Drain. Cool. ■ Alternate pieces of rutabaga, pineapple, red onion and pork on each skewer. ■ Sauté onion and jalapeños in oil in medium skillet until onion is soft. Purée remaining 6 ingredients. Stir into onion mixture. Simmer over low for 20 minutes. Preheat barbecue to medium low. Place skewers on greased grill. Close lid. Cook for 25 to 30 minutes, turning and basting with sauce several times, until desired doneness. Reheat remaining sauce to boiling before serving. Makes 6 skewers.

1 skewer: 217 Calories; 4 g Total Fat; 110 mg Sodium; 12 g Protein; 37 g Carbohydrate; 4 g Dietary Fiber

Note: When chopping chili peppers use gloves, as the caustic oily compounds, called capsaicin (kap-SAY-ih-sihn), permeate the skin and can cause a burning sensation.

Exotic Pork Saté

Melt in your mouth tender with pleasant ginger flavor. Serve with Chili Peanut Sauce, page 21. Pictured on front cover.

Lean boneless pork loin, trimmed of surface fat, cut into $^3/_4$ inch (2 cm) cubes	**1 lb.**	**454 g**
Garlic cloves, minced	**4**	**4**
Finely grated gingerroot	**2 tsp.**	**10 mL**
Anchovy paste	**1 tbsp.**	**15 mL**
Dark soy sauce	**3 tbsp.**	**50 mL**
Prepared orange juice	**2 tbsp.**	**30 mL**
Worcestershire sauce	**1 tbsp.**	**15 mL**
Lemon juice	**1 tbsp.**	**15 mL**
Coriander seeds, crushed	**2 tsp.**	**10 mL**
Turmeric	**$^1/_2$ tsp.**	**2 mL**
10 inch (25 cm) bamboo skewers, soaked in water for 10 minutes	**6**	**6**

Place pork in sealable plastic bag or shallow casserole. ■ Whisk next 9 ingredients together in small bowl. Makes 6 tbsp. (100 mL) marinade. Pour over pork. Seal bag. Marinate in refrigerator for 3 to 4 hours or overnight, stirring several times. ■ Preheat lightly sprayed electric grill to medium-high. Push 8 to 10 cubes onto each skewer. Brush with marinade. Discard remaining marinade. Cook skewers for 2 to 3 minutes per side until desired doneness. Makes 6 skewers.

1 skewer: 81 Calories; 2.2 g Total Fat; 634 mg Sodium; 12 g Protein; 3 g Carbohydrate; trace Dietary Fiber

Variation: Use 4 inch (10 cm) skewers. Place 3 pork cubes on each for appetizers. Makes 18 to 20 small appetizer skewers.

....

Once food has touched the greased grill, don't move or shift it around until it's time to turn it. This should help prevent sticking and will promote nice, even grill marks. Starting with a cleaned grill is also recommended.

Tenderloin Saté

Wonderful aroma when cooking. The flavor of spices really comes through. The fat comes from the coconut milk.

Canned coconut milk	14 oz.	400 mL
Lemon juice	$^1/_2$ tsp.	2 mL
Garlic clove, minced	1	1
Grated onion	2 tsp.	10 mL
Curry paste	1 tsp.	5 mL
Granulated sugar	1 tsp.	5 mL
Ground cumin	$^1/_2$ tsp.	2 mL
Ground coriander	$^1/_2$ tsp.	2 mL
Salt	$^1/_4$ tsp.	1 mL
Ground cinnamon, just a pinch		
Pork tenderloin, cut into 1 inch (2.5 cm) cubes (about 20 chunks)	2 lbs.	900 g
8 inch (20 cm) bamboo skewers, soaked in water for 10 minutes	10	10

Whisk first 10 ingredients together in medium bowl. Makes 1$^2/_3$ cups (400 mL) marinade. ■ Put pork cubes into marinade. Cover. Marinate in refrigerator for 2 hours. ■ Preheat lightly sprayed electric grill to medium. Push cubes close together onto skewers. Cook on grill for about 15 minutes, turning and basting with marinade several times, until cooked. Discard any remaining marinade. Makes 10 skewers.

1 skewer: 301 Calories; 20.8 g Total Fat; 171 mg Sodium; 26 g Protein; 3 g Carbohydrate; trace Dietary Fiber

Sesame Pork Balls

A unique way of doing pork balls. The sesame seeds give a nice look. Pictured on page 54.

Lean ground pork	1 lb.	454 g
Large egg, fork-beaten	1	1
Fine dry bread crumbs	$^1/_2$ cup	125 mL
Garlic cloves, minced	2	2
Sliced green onion	$^1/_3$ cup	75 mL
Low-sodium soy sauce	1 tbsp.	15 mL
Cayenne pepper	$^1/_4$ tsp.	1 mL
Salt	$^1/_2$ tsp.	2 mL
Freshly ground pepper, sprinkle		
Sesame seeds	$^1/_2$ cup	125 mL
Long double-pronged metal skewers	4	4

(continued on next page)

Combine first 9 ingredients in medium bowl until well mixed. Form into 16 balls, about 1³/₄ inches (4.5 cm) wide. ■ Roll balls in sesame seeds. ■ Preheat lightly sprayed electric grill to medium-high. Push 4 balls onto each skewer. Cook for 16 to 18 minutes, turning frequently to cook all sides, until balls are no longer pink inside. Makes 4 skewers.

1 skewer: 316 Calories; 18.8 g Total Fat; 665 mg Sodium; 24 g Protein; 14 g Carbohydrate; 1 g Dietary Fiber

Scallop And Vegetable Skewers

When you want to impress company serve these skewers with wild rice. Pictured on front cover.

Medium zucchini, with peel, cut into ¹/₄ inch (6 mm) lengthwise slices	**3**	**3**
Boiling water	**3 qts.**	**3 L**
Long double-pronged metal skewers	**6**	**6**
Medium red pepper, seeded and diced into 1 inch (2.5 cm) pieces	**1**	**1**
Sea scallops (about 1 lb., 454 g)	**18**	**18**
Medium yellow pepper, seeded and diced into 1 inch (2.5 cm) pieces	**1**	**1**
Italian dressing (see Note)	**³/₄ cup**	**175 mL**
Balsamic vinegar	**1¹/₂ tsp.**	**7 mL**
Dried sweet basil	**1 tsp.**	**5 mL**

Blanch zucchini slices in boiling water in large saucepan for 30 to 40 seconds. ■ Push skewer through end of 1 zucchini slice. Push on red pepper piece. Zig-zag zucchini slice back and forth over alternating scallop and yellow pepper piece. May need more than 1 slice of zucchini per skewer. Repeat for remaining skewers. ■ Combine dressing, vinegar and basil in small bowl. Makes ³/₄ cup (175 mL) marinade. Set aside ¹/₄ cup (60 mL) for basting. Pour remaining marinade into large sealable plastic bag set on large plate. Slide in skewers and turn to coat. Seal bag. Marinate in refrigerator for several hours or overnight. Drain and discard marinade. Preheat lightly sprayed electric grill to medium. Cook skewers on grill for 15 minutes, turning and basting frequently with reserved marinade, until scallops are opaque and firm. Discard any remaining marinade. Makes 6 skewers.

1 skewer: 230 Calories; 16.8 g Total Fat; 492 mg Sodium; 14 g Protein; 7 g Carbohydrate; 2 g Dietary Fiber

Note: Non-fat Italian dressing can be substituted but it will have a "bite" that overpowers the more delicate flavor of the seafood.

Rosemary Scallops

These delicate scallops make a wonderful appetizer. You may need to visit your favorite fish market to get the large scallops or phone ahead to order them. Pictured on page 143.

White (or alcohol-free white) wine	$^1/_2$ cup	125 mL
Lemon juice	2 tbsp.	30 mL
Chopped fresh rosemary leaves	$^1/_2$-1 tsp.	2-5 mL
Freshly ground pepper, sprinkle		
Sea scallops (about 2 inches, 5 cm, in diameter)	12	12
8 inch (20 cm) bamboo skewers, soaked in water for 10 minutes	4	4
Olive oil	1 tbsp.	15 mL
Fresh rosemary sprigs (about 5 inches, 12.5 cm, long)	4	4

Combine first 4 ingredients in medium bowl. Makes $^2/_3$ cup (150 mL) marinade. ■ Add scallops. Marinate at room temperature for 30 minutes, stirring gently once or twice. ■ Preheat lightly sprayed electric grill to medium-high. Drain and discard marinade. Push 3 scallops, from edge to edge through diameter, onto each skewer. ■ Lay gently on grill. Cook for about 2 minutes per side, basting with olive oil, until opaque and firm. ■ Remove leaves from rosemary sprigs, leaving a few leaves on top end for appearance. Carefully remove skewers from scallops and replace with rosemary sprigs. Makes 4 skewers.

1 skewer: 116 Calories; 4.1 g Total Fat; 122 mg Sodium; 13 g Protein; 3 g Carbohydrate; trace Dietary Fiber

Hazelnut Halibut

The toasted hazelnuts give these skewers a lovely crunchy texture (but also be aware that they add fat grams). Nice lemon finish. Pictured on page 144.

Halibut, cut into 1$^1/_2$ inch (3.8 cm) cubes	1$^1/_4$ lbs.	560 g
Long flat-sided metal skewers	4	4
Thin lemon slices (about 2 lemons)	20	20
Tub margarine, melted	$^1/_4$ cup	60 mL
Freshly ground pepper, sprinkle		
Finely chopped hazelnuts	1 cup	250 mL

(continued on next page)

Preheat lightly sprayed electric grill to high. Push halibut cubes onto skewers, with folded lemon slice between each piece. ■ Brush fish and lemon with melted margarine. Sprinkle with pepper. ■ Spread hazelnuts on waxed paper. Roll skewers in hazelnuts to evenly coat fish on all sides. Place skewers on grill. Cook for about 10 minutes, turning several times, until fish is opaque and hazelnuts are toasted. Makes 4 skewers.

1 skewer: 454 Calories; 33.5 g Total Fat; 227 mg Sodium; 34 g Protein; 7 g Carbohydrate; 2 g Dietary Fiber

Shrimp Butterflies

Garlicy good!

Freshly squeezed lemon juice	$^1/_4$ **cup**	**60 mL**
Finely grated lemon peel	$^1/_2$ **tsp.**	**2 mL**
Garlic cloves, minced	**3**	**3**
Low-sodium soy sauce	**2 tbsp.**	**30 mL**
Sherry (or alcohol-free sherry)	**2 tbsp.**	**30 mL**
Canola oil	**1 tbsp.**	**15 mL**
Large fresh (or frozen, thawed) raw tiger shrimp (21-25 count)	**1 lb.**	**454 g**
6 inch (15 cm) bamboo skewers, soaked in water for 10 minutes	**8**	**8**

Combine first 6 ingredients in medium bowl. Makes $^1/_2$ cup (125 mL) marinade. ■ Peel and devein shrimp, leaving tails intact. Make deep cut along outside spine of shrimp, almost but not through to other side. Stir shrimp into marinade. Marinate in refrigerator for 30 minutes. Drain and reserve marinade. ■ Preheat lightly sprayed electric grill to high. Push shrimp onto skewers through tail to make a curl. Cook for 3 to 4 minutes, turning and basting with reserved marinade, until shrimp are pink and firm. Discard any remaining marinade. Makes 8 skewers.

1 skewer: 82 Calories; 2.6 g Total Fat; 225 mg Sodium; 12 g Protein; 2 g Carbohydrate; trace Dietary Fiber

Variation: Soft fruits or vegetables, such as cherry tomatoes, mango and peach chunks can be placed between shrimp if desired.

Fruited Seafood Grill

A fish lover's delight.

Juice and 1 tsp. (5 mL) finely grated peel of 1 medium orange		
Canned fruit cocktail, with juice	14 oz.	398 mL
Pink grapefruit cocktail drink box	1 cup	250 mL
Fresh rosemary leaves	2 tsp.	10 mL
Canola oil	1 tbsp.	15 mL
Small garlic clove, minced	1	1
Salmon fillet, cut into 1¹/₂ inch (3.8 cm) cubes	¹/₂ lb.	225 g
Fresh (or frozen, thawed) sea scallops	¹/₂ lb.	225 g
Large fresh (or frozen, thawed) raw shrimp, peeled and deveined	¹/₂ lb.	225 g
10 inch (25 cm) bamboo skewers, soaked in water for 10 minutes	6	6
Seedless red grapes, approximately	40	40

Blend first 6 ingredients until smooth. Makes 3¹/₄ cups (800 mL) marinade. Pour ¹/₂ of marinade into medium bowl. Reserve remainder for basting. ■ Add fish and seafood to marinade in bowl. Cover. Marinate in refrigerator for 3 hours or longer. ■ Preheat lightly sprayed electric grill to high. Push alternating pieces of seafood and grapes onto skewers. Discard any marinade remaining in bowl. Cook skewers for about 6 minutes, turning and basting frequently with reserved marinade, until salmon and seafood are cooked. Discard any remaining marinade. Makes 6 skewers.

1 skewer: 207 Calories; 4.5 g Total Fat; 148 mg Sodium; 22 g Protein; 21 g Carbohydrate; 2 g Dietary Fiber

Peppered Lobster Skewers

When you're feeling extravagant try this delectable recipe.

Plain yogurt (or strained)	1 cup	250 mL
Olive oil	1 tbsp.	15 mL
Whole black peppercorns, cracked in plastic bag with mallet	1 tbsp.	15 mL
Salt	1 tsp.	5 mL
Lobster tail meat (raw, removed from shell), cut into 1 inch (2.5 cm) pieces	1 lb.	454 g
6 inch (15 cm) bamboo skewers, soaked in water for 10 minutes	4	4

(continued on next page)

Combine first 4 ingredients in medium bowl. ■ Gently stir in lobster pieces to coat. Cover. Marinate in refrigerator for 1 hour, stirring twice. ■ Preheat lightly sprayed electric grill to medium-high. Remove lobster and discard marinade. Push lobster chunks onto skewers. Cook for about 8 minutes, turning several times. Makes 4 skewers.

1 skewer: 157 Calories; 4.3 g Total Fat; 879 mg Sodium; 24 g Protein; 5 g Carbohydrate; trace Dietary Fiber

Variation: Halibut, haddock or any firm fish can be substituted for the more expensive lobster.

Lemon Garlic Shrimp

What could be nicer than lemon and garlic with shrimp!

Freshly squeezed lemon juice	2 tbsp.	30 mL
Finely grated lemon peel	$1/2$ tsp.	2 mL
Garlic cloves, minced	4	4
Olive oil	$1/4$ cup	60 mL
Chopped fresh parsley	2 tbsp.	30 mL
Dry mustard	1 tsp.	5 mL
Cayenne pepper	$1/4$ tsp.	1 mL
Medium fresh (or frozen, thawed) raw shrimp (34 count), peeled and deveined, tails intact (about 16)	$1/2$ lb.	225 g
6 inch (15 cm) bamboo skewers, soaked in water for 10 minutes	4	4

Combine first 7 ingredients in medium bowl. Makes scant $1/2$ cup (125 mL) marinade. ■ Add shrimp. Toss well to coat. Marinate in refrigerator for 30 minutes. ■ Preheat lightly sprayed electric grill to high. Push 4 shrimp onto each skewer. Discard any remaining marinade. Cook on grill for 1 minute per side until shrimp are pink and firm. Makes 4 skewers.

1 skewer: 179 Calories; 13.6 g Total Fat; 85 mg Sodium; 12 g Protein; 2 g Carbohydrate; trace Dietary Fiber

Rainbow Skewers

The name says it all. Gorgeous!

Medium red pepper, seeded and cut into 1¹/₂ inch (3.8 cm) squares	1	1
Medium yellow pepper, seeded and cut into 1¹/₂ inch (3.8 cm) squares	1	1
Red onion, wedged	1	1
Medium zucchini, quartered lengthwise and then cut into 1¹/₂ inch (3.8 cm) pieces	1	1
Non-fat Italian dressing	²/₃ cup	150 mL
Garlic clove, minced	1	1
Freshly ground pepper, generous sprinkle		
10 inch (25 cm) bamboo skewers, soaked in water for 10 minutes	4	4

Place vegetables in large bowl. ■ Combine dressing, garlic and pepper in small bowl. Makes ²/₃ cup (150 mL) marinade. Add to vegetables. Stir to coat. Marinate in refrigerator for 1 to 2 hours, stirring several times to coat vegetables. ■ Preheat lightly sprayed electric grill to high. Drain and reserve marinade. Alternate vegetables on skewers. Cook for 12 minutes, turning several times and basting with reserved marinade several times, until vegetables are tender-crisp. Discard any remaining marinade. Makes 4 skewers.

1 skewer: 39 Calories; 0.2 g Total Fat; 428 mg Sodium; 1 g Protein; 9 g Carbohydrate; 2 g Dietary Fiber

Onion Sticks

A pleasant taste of thyme and vinegar mingle with the onion. Pictured on page 125.

Rice vinegar	2 tbsp.	30 mL
Olive oil	1 tbsp.	15 mL
Cooking molasses	1 tbsp.	15 mL
Finely chopped fresh thyme leaves	2 tsp.	10 mL
Large Spanish onion, quartered lengthwise and then cut crosswise, layers separated	1	1
4 inch (10 cm) bamboo skewers, soaked in water for 10 minutes	6	6
Fresh thyme sprigs	12	12

(continued on next page)

Combine first 4 ingredients in medium bowl. Makes ¹/₄ cup (60 mL) marinade.
■ Add onion pieces. Toss to coat. Cover. Marinate in refrigerator overnight. ■ Preheat barbecue to medium. Push onion pieces onto skewers, alternating sprigs of thyme in 2 or 3 places along skewer. Drain and reserve marinade. Place skewers on greased grill. Close lid. Cook for about 20 minutes, turning and basting frequently with reserved marinade, until onion is soft and golden. Discard any remaining marinade. Makes 6 skewers.

1 skewer: 42 Calories; 2.3 g Total Fat; 2 mg Sodium; trace Protein; 6 g Carbohydrate; 1 g Dietary Fiber

Curried Vegetables

The apple and curry flavors really come through. Pictured on page 108.

Medium carrots, cut into 1¹/₂ inch (3.8 cm) lengths	**4**	**4**
Simmering water	**2 cups**	**500 mL**
Cauliflower florets, about 1¹/₂-2 inches (3.8-5 cm) in diameter	**1 lb.**	**454 g**
Medium zucchini, with peel, cut into 1¹/₂ inch (3.8 cm) pieces	**2**	**2**
Long double-pronged metal skewers	**4**	**4**
Large onion, cut into large dice	**1**	**1**
Apple juice	**2 tbsp.**	**30 mL**
Apple jelly preserves	**2 tbsp.**	**30 mL**
Chutney, larger pieces chopped fine	**¹/₄ cup**	**60 mL**
Curry paste	**¹/₂ tsp.**	**2 mL**

Steam carrot pieces over simmering water in large saucepan for 5 to 7 minutes until tender-crisp. Cool. ■ Steam cauliflower florets over same simmering water in same large saucepan for 4 to 6 minutes until just tender-crisp. Cool. ■ Steam zucchini pieces over same simmering water in same large saucepan for 2 to 3 minutes until tender-crisp. ■ Alternate vegetable pieces and onion pieces on each skewer. ■ Preheat barbecue to medium. Combine remaining 4 ingredients in small saucepan. Warm until jelly is dissolved. Makes 6 tbsp. (100 mL) basting sauce. Place skewers on greased grill. Close lid. Cook for about 15 minutes, turning and basting with sauce several times, until vegetables are soft and glazed. Serve remaining sauce with vegetables. Makes 4 skewers.

1 skewer: 135 Calories; 0.8 g Total Fat; 51 mg Sodium; 4 g Protein; 31 g Carbohydrate; 6 g Dietary Fiber

Buttered Potatoes

Who said potatoes had to be boring.

Large Russet potatoes, with skin scrubbed (approx. ³/₄ lb., 340 g)	2	2
Large sweet potato, with skin scrubbed (about ³/₄ lb., 340 g)	1	1
Long flat-sided metal skewers	4	4
Tub margarine	¹/₄ **cup**	**60 mL**
Chopped fresh parsley	1 tbsp.	15 mL
Salt	1 tsp.	5 mL
Freshly ground pepper, sprinkle		

Cut both kinds of potatoes into similar size chunks, about 1 inch (2.5 cm) in size. Rinse with cold water. Drain. Microwave in large bowl, covered with plastic wrap, on high (100%) for about 5 minutes until partially cooked. Let cool slightly. ■ Arrange alternating pieces of white and sweet potatoes on each skewer. ■ Melt margarine in small saucepan. Stir in remaining 3 ingredients. Preheat lightly sprayed electric grill to high. Brush margarine mixture over potatoes on all sides and place on grill. Cook for 8 to 10 minutes, turning and basting several times with margarine mixture, until fork tender. Makes 4 skewers.

1 skewer: 197 Calories; 12.2 g Total Fat; 849 mg Sodium; 2 g Protein; 20 g Carbohydrate; 2 g Dietary Fiber

Potatoes On A Stick

The first potatoes of the season are memorable when prepared this way. Pictured on page 18.

New baby red potatoes	10	10
New baby white potatoes	10	10
Water	2 cups	500 mL
Olive oil	2 tbsp.	30 mL
Seasoned salt	1 tsp.	5 mL
Dried sweet basil	¹/₂ tsp.	2 mL
Dried whole oregano	¹/₂ tsp.	2 mL
Ground rosemary	¹/₈ tsp.	0.5 mL
Freshly ground pepper, sprinkle		
Long flat-sided metal skewers	4	4

(continued on next page)

Preheat lightly sprayed electric grill to high. Par-boil potatoes in water in medium saucepan for 5 minutes. Drain well. Cool enough to handle. ■ Combine next 6 ingredients in small bowl. ■ Push potatoes, alternating red and white, onto skewers. Brush potatoes on all sides with olive oil mixture. Cook for about 30 minutes, turning and basting several times, until tender. Makes 4 skewers.

1 skewer: 191 Calories; 7.1 g Total Fat; 347 mg Sodium; 3 g Protein; 30 g Carbohydrate; 3 g Dietary Fiber

Lamb Kabobs

Full meal on a skewer. What could be easier. Pictured on page 107.

Low-fat Italian dressing	1/4 **cup**	60 mL
Chopped fresh mint leaves, packed	2 tbsp.	30 mL
White wine vinegar	1 tbsp.	15 mL
Lean lamb, cut into 3/4 inch (2 cm) cubes	1/2 **lb.**	225 g
Baby red potatoes, with peel	8	8
Water, to just cover		
Salt	1/2 **tsp.**	2 mL
HERB AND MINT SAUCE		
Low-fat Italian dressing	1/2 **cup**	125 mL
Mint jelly	1/4 **cup**	60 mL
Small zucchini slices, cut 3/4 inch (2 cm) thick	8	8
Small roma (plum) tomatoes, quartered	2	2
Large sweet onion, cut into 8 chunks	1	1
Long metal skewers	4	4

Combine first 3 ingredients in medium bowl. Makes 1/3 cup (75 mL) marinade. Stir in lamb cubes. Cover. Marinate in refrigerator for several hours or overnight. Drain and discard marinade. ■ Par-boil potatoes in water and salt in small saucepan for 10 to 15 minutes until tender when poked with tip of knife. Drain and cool. ■ **Herb And Mint Sauce:** Combine dressing and mint jelly in small bowl. Warm slightly in microwave, if necessary to blend. ■ Preheat barbecue to medium. Alternate vegetables and lamb cubes on each skewer. Place skewers on greased grill. Close lid. Cook for 15 to 20 minutes, turning and basting with sauce several times, until desired doneness. Reheat remaining sauce to boiling before serving with kabobs. Makes 4 skewers.

1 skewer: 229 Calories; 4.7 g Total Fat; 715 mg Sodium; 14 g Protein; 34 g Carbohydrate; 3 g Dietary Fiber

Souvlaki

The lamb can be prepared the night before and left in the refrigerator to marinate. Pictured on page 18.

Olive oil	$^1/_4$ **cup**	60 mL
Lemon juice	**2 tbsp.**	30 mL
Chopped fresh oregano leaves	**2 tbsp.**	30 mL
Bay leaves	**2**	2
Freshly ground pepper	$^1/_4$ **tsp.**	1 mL
Lamb, trimmed of visible fat, cut into $1^1/_2$ **inch (3.8 cm) cubes**	**1 lb.**	454 g
Medium mild (or red) onions, cut into **1 inch (2.5 cm) pieces**	**2**	2
Medium green peppers, seeded and cut into $1^1/_2$ **inch (3.8 cm) chunks**	**2**	2
Long flat-sided metal skewers	**12**	12
Medium whole fresh mushrooms	**12**	12
Cherry tomatoes	**12**	12

Combine olive oil, lemon juice, oregano, bay leaves and pepper in shallow glass pan or casserole. Makes about $^1/_3$ cup (75 mL) marinade. ■ Add lamb. Cover. Marinate in refrigerator for at least 5 hours or overnight, turning several times to coat. Discard bay leaves. ■ Add onion pieces and green pepper chunks. Toss to coat. ■ Preheat lightly sprayed electric grill to medium-high. Drain and reserve marinade for basting. Alternate lamb, pepper chunks and onion pieces on each skewer. Place mushroom at end of each skewer, leaving enough room to add cherry tomato after. Cook for about 15 minutes, turning and basting several times with reserved marinade. ■ Place cherry tomatoes on tips of skewers. Cook for 5 minutes until desired doneness. Discard any remaining marinade. Makes 12 skewers.

1 skewer: 106 Calories; 6.3 g Total Fat; 24 mg Sodium; 9 g Protein; 4 g Carbohydrate; 1 g Dietary Fiber

....

To make removal of cooked meat easier, lightly oil skewers (metal or wooden) before adding meat or fish. Brush oil on with a basting brush, then wipe gently with a paper towel to remove excess.

Two-Sided Grilling

n this section you will find a variety of excellent recipes using a two-sided or full contact grill. The recipes are unique and interesting besides being delicious. Experience mouthwatering stir-fry or delicious guilt-free potato pancakes, cooked on a grill. These grills are ideally suited for smaller families or for two people.

Italian Focaccia Sandwiches

A sandwich never tasted so good. Substitute lean ham for the prosciutto to lower the fat grams.

Focaccia bread (10 inch, 25 cm, size)	1	1
Sun-dried tomato pesto	2 tbsp.	30 mL
Thin slices provolone cheese (about 6 oz., 170 g)	12	12
Paper-thin slices red onion	6	6
Paper-thin slices prosciutto (about 12 oz., 340 g)	12	12
Diced green pepper	6 tbsp.	100 mL
Non-fat Italian dressing	6 tbsp.	100 mL

Preheat lightly sprayed 2-sided electric grill for 5 minutes. Split focaccia in half horizontally. Spread each cut side with thin coating of pesto. ■ Place 6 slices of cheese over pesto on bottom half only. Layer red onion and prosciutto over cheese. Sprinkle green pepper over all. ■ Drizzle with dressing. Top with remaining 6 slices of cheese. Cover with top half of focaccia. Cut into 8 wedges. Place 2 wedges on grill. Close lid. Cook for 5 minutes until bread is toasted and cheese is melted inside. Repeat with remaining wedges. Makes 8 sandwiches.

1 sandwich: 567 Calories; 41.5 g Total Fat; 1252 mg Sodium; 13 g Protein; 34 g Carbohydrate; 1 g Dietary Fiber

Easy Monte Cristo Sandwiches

A tried-and-true sandwich made easier.

French bread slices, cut ¹/₂ inch (12 mm) thick	**8**	**8**
Thin slices Swiss cheese (about 4 oz., 113 g)	**4**	**4**
Shaved deli turkey	**4 oz.**	**113 g**
Freshly ground pepper, sprinkle		
Tomato slices	**8**	**8**
Salt, sprinkle		
Thin slices Swiss cheese (about 4 oz., 113 g)	**4**	**4**
Shaved deli ham	**4 oz.**	**113 g**
Sliced green onion	**¹/₂ cup**	**125 mL**
Thin slices Swiss cheese (about 4 oz., 113 g)	**4**	**4**
Large eggs, fork-beaten	**4**	**4**
Milk	**¹/₂ cup**	**125 mL**
Salt, sprinkle		

Preheat lightly sprayed 2-sided electric grill for 5 minutes. Layer 4 bread slices with next 9 ingredients in order given. Top with remaining 4 bread slices. ■ Combine eggs, milk and salt in shallow dish that will hold all sandwiches. Turn sandwiches in egg mixture to soak completely. Place 2 sandwiches on grill. Close lid. Cook for 5 minutes. Repeat with remaining 2 sandwiches. Makes 4 sandwiches.

1 sandwich: 637 Calories; 31.9 g Total Fat; 1013 mg Sodium; 50 g Protein; 35 g Carbohydrate; 1 g Dietary Fiber

1. Onion Sticks, page 118
2. Potato Pancakes (with side dish of applesauce), page 137
3. Grilled Peperonata, page 150

Open-Faced Chicken Sandwiches

Serve these with a bowl of hearty soup for a full meal.

Focaccia bread (10 inch, 25 cm, size)	**1**	**1**
Boneless, skinless chicken breast halves (about 4)	**1 lb.**	**454 g**
Sliced fresh mushrooms	**2 cups**	**500 mL**
Chopped onion	**1 cup**	**250 mL**
Garlic cloves, minced	**4**	**4**
Finely chopped fresh rosemary leaves	**1 tsp.**	**5 mL**
Chopped fresh marjoram leaves	**1 tsp.**	**5 mL**
Salt	**¹/₄ tsp.**	**1 mL**
Pepper	**¹/₈ tsp.**	**0.5 mL**
All-purpose flour	**4 tsp.**	**20 mL**
Light cream cheese, diced into small cubes	**8 oz.**	**250 g**
Grated part-skim mozzarella cheese	**1¹/₃ cups**	**325 mL**

Preheat lightly sprayed 2-sided electric grill for 5 minutes. Split focaccia bread in half horizontally. Cut each half into 6 wedges, for a total of 12. ■ Cut chicken into small bite-size cubes. Combine chicken, mushrooms, onion, garlic, rosemary and marjoram in medium bowl. Toss well. Turn out onto grill. Close lid. Cook for 5 to 8 minutes until chicken is no longer pink inside and onion is soft. ■ Sprinkle with salt, pepper, flour and both cheeses. Close lid. Cook for 2 minutes. Carefully lift and divide chicken mixture over bread wedges. Place 2 wedges on grill. Close lid. Grill for 2 minutes. Repeat with remaining wedges. Makes 12 open-faced sandwiches.

1 sandwich: 238 Calories; 6.7 g Total Fat; 541 mg Sodium; 18 g Protein; 25 g Carbohydrate; 1 g Dietary Fiber

Variation: Use 2 focaccia breads. Cut each into 6 wedges. Split each wedge in half horizontally. Open as for sandwiches. Divide chicken mixture over 12 bottom wedges. Cover with remaining 12 top wedges. Place 2 sandwiches on grill. Close lid. Cook for 2 minutes. Makes 12 topped sandwiches instead of open-faced.

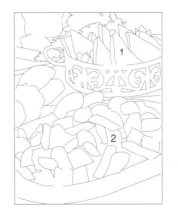

1. Confetti Polenta Wedges, page 129
2. Warm Penne And Vegetables, page 138

Fast Seafood Pasta

Lots of color with showy bow tie pasta. Lots of seafood makes this an exceptional recipe for company.

Bow tie (or other medium) pasta (about 8 oz., 225 g)	2²/₃ cups	650 mL
Boiling water	12 cups	3 L
Salt	1 tbsp.	15 mL
Chopped onion	¹/₄ cup	60 mL
Diced celery	¹/₄ cup	60 mL
Chopped fresh mushrooms	¹/₂ cup	125 mL
Garlic clove, minced	1	1
Diced red pepper	¹/₂ cup	125 mL
Diced zucchini, with peel	¹/₂ cup	125 mL
Chili sauce	¹/₄ cup	60 mL
Frozen medium raw shrimp (about 8 oz., 225 g)	1¹/₂ cups	375 mL
Frozen bay (small) scallops (about 8 oz., 225 g)	1 cup	250 mL
Canola oil	2 tsp.	10 mL
Chopped fresh sweet basil (or 2 tsp., 10 mL, dried)	2 tbsp.	30 mL
Chopped fresh parsley (or 1 tsp., 5 mL, dried)	1 tbsp.	15 mL
Cayenne pepper, sprinkle		
Salt	¹/₄ tsp.	1 mL
Freshly ground pepper, generous sprinkle		

Preheat lightly sprayed 2-sided electric grill for 5 minutes. Cook pasta in boiling water and first amount of salt in large pot or Dutch oven for 7 to 9 minutes until tender. Drain well. Return pasta to pot to keep warm. ■ Toss next 7 ingredients together in small bowl. Set aside. ■ Toss frozen shrimp, scallops, oil, basil, parsley, cayenne pepper, second amount of salt and pepper together in large bowl. Turn out vegetable mixture onto grill. Close lid. Cook for 3 minutes. Add seafood mixture. Close lid. Cook for 7 minutes. Toss seafood-vegetable mixture with pasta, plus juices from drip tray under grill. Makes 6¹/₂ cups (1.6 L), enough for 4 servings.

1 serving: 374 Calories; 4.8 g Total Fat; 600 mg Sodium; 29 g Protein; 52 g Carbohydrate; 4 g Dietary Fiber

Confetti Polenta Wedges

Very attractive with flecks of green and red pepper showing. Pictured on page 126.

Tub margarine	1 tbsp.	15 mL
Finely chopped green onion	1/4 cup	60 mL
Finely chopped red pepper	1/4 cup	60 mL
Coarsely grated carrot	1/4 cup	60 mL
Condensed chicken broth	10 oz.	284 mL
Milk	1 cup	250 mL
Freshly ground pepper, sprinkle		
Yellow cornmeal	1 cup	250 mL
Olive oil, for brushing	1 tbsp.	15 mL
Grated strong-flavored cheese (such as Parmesan, sharp Cheddar or provolone)	2 tbsp.	30 mL

Heat margarine in large non-stick wok or skillet. Sauté green onion, red pepper and carrot for 2 minutes. ■ Stir in broth, milk and pepper. Heat to simmering. ■ Slowly add cornmeal, stirring constantly. Stir constantly for 5 to 10 minutes until polenta is very thick and pulling away from sides of wok. Pour into greased 9 inch (22 cm) round cake pan. Let cool and stiffen. ■ Preheat lightly sprayed 2-sided electric grill for 5 minutes. Turn polenta out onto cutting board. Brush both sides with olive oil. Cut into 8 wedges. Place 4 wedges on grill. Close lid. Cook for 5 to 8 minutes until crispy and browned. Repeat with remaining wedges. ■ Sprinkle each wedge with cheese while hot. Serve immediately. Makes 8 wedges.

1 wedge: 129 Calories; 4.6 g Total Fat; 297 mg Sodium; 5 g Protein; 17 g Carbohydrate; 1 g Dietary Fiber

· ·

Assemble all your grilling items—food, utensils, basting sauce—on a tray before heading out to the barbecue. Not only will this save you some time running back and forth to fetch things, but you will also be able to stay and keep a close eye on flare-ups, and maybe avoid overcooking.

Stirless Stir-Fry

A different way to prepare a traditional dish! Serve this over rice. Pictured on page 71.

Boneless, skinless chicken breast halves (about 3)	³/₄ **lb.**	**340 g**
Garlic cloves, minced	**2**	**2**
Medium carrot, thinly sliced on diagonal	**1**	**1**
Thinly sliced celery, cut on diagonal	¹/₂ **cup**	**125 mL**
Slivered green pepper	¹/₂ **cup**	**125 mL**
Small onion, cut lengthwise into wedges	**1**	**1**
Fresh bean sprouts	**2 cups**	**500 mL**
Cornstarch	**2 tsp.**	**10 mL**
Water	¹/₂ **cup**	**125 mL**
Chicken (or vegetable) bouillon powder	**1 tbsp.**	**15 mL**
Low-sodium soy sauce	**1 tbsp.**	**15 mL**
Ground ginger	¹/₂ **tsp.**	**2 mL**
Granulated sugar	¹/₂ **tsp.**	**2 mL**
Dried crushed chilies	¹/₄ **tsp.**	**1 mL**

Preheat lightly sprayed 2-sided electric grill for 5 minutes. Combine chicken and garlic in small bowl. Turn out onto grill. Close lid. Cook for 5 minutes. Remove to bowl. ■ Place next 5 ingredients on grill. Close lid. Cook for 5 minutes until vegetables are tender-crisp. ■ Combine remaining 7 ingredients in large saucepan. Cook, stirring frequently, until boiling and thickened. Add chicken and vegetables. Stir to coat. Makes 4 cups (1 L).

1 cup (250 mL): 164 Calories; 2.9 g Total Fat; 719 mg Sodium; 23 g Protein; 11 g Carbohydrate; 2 g Dietary Fiber

Chicken Cordon Swiss Patties

Serve on a grilled Kaiser bun and garnish with condiments of your choice.

Lean ground chicken (white meat)	**1 lb.**	**454 g**
Large egg, fork-beaten	**1**	**1**
Fine dry bread crumbs	¹/₃ **cup**	**75 mL**
Onion salt	¹/₂ **tsp.**	**2 mL**
Parsley flakes	**1 tsp.**	**5 mL**
Thin slices Black Forest ham	**3 oz.**	**85 g**
Grated Gruyère cheese	¹/₂ **cup**	**125 mL**

(continued on next page)

Preheat lightly sprayed 2-sided electric grill for 5 minutes. Combine first 5 ingredients in medium bowl. Form into 8 equal-size portions. Flatten 4 portions into 3¹/₂ inch (9 cm) patties. ■ Place thin slice of ham (cut to fit) and grated Gruyère cheese on top of each patty. Top each with remaining patties. Seal edges by pressing together very well. Place 2 patties on grill. Cook for 8 to 10 minutes until chicken is no longer pink. Makes 4 patties.

1 patty: 268 Calories; 8.8 g Total Fat; 681 mg Sodium; 37g Protein 8 g Carbohydrate; trace Dietary Fiber

Vegetarian Chili On A Bun

A green salad served with this makes a complete meal. Pictured on page 90.

Chopped onion	**¹/₂ cup**	**125 mL**
Chopped celery	**¹/₂ cup**	**125 mL**
Chopped fresh parsley	**2 tbsp.**	**30 mL**
Chopped unsalted peanuts (optional)	**¹/₂ cup**	**125 mL**
Canned diced tomatoes, drained and juice reserved	**14 oz.**	**398 mL**
Canned red kidney beans, drained and rinsed	**14 oz.**	**398 mL**
Brown sugar, packed	**¹/₂ tsp.**	**2 mL**
Chili powder	**1 tsp.**	**5 mL**
Freshly ground pepper, sprinkle		
Garlic clove, minced	**1**	**1**
Coriander seeds, crushed	**1 tsp.**	**5 mL**
Ground cumin	**¹/₂ tsp.**	**2 mL**
Paprika	**1 tsp.**	**5 mL**
Reserved tomato juice		
Whole wheat buns, split and toasted	**2**	**2**
Grated medium Cheddar cheese, for garnish		

Preheat lightly sprayed 2-sided electric grill for 5 minutes. Toss first 13 ingredients together in large bowl. Turn out contents of bowl onto grill. Close lid. Cook for 10 minutes until onion is soft. ■ Return contents to bowl. Stir in reserved tomato juice along with contents of drip tray from grill. Makes 2¹/₂ cups (625 mL). ■ Serve chili over top of bun halves. Sprinkle with cheese. Serves 2.

1 serving: 302 Calories; 2.7 g Total Fat; 1135 mg Sodium; 15 g Protein; 60 g Carbohydrate; 16 g Dietary Fiber

Rolled Sole With Sesame

An interesting way to present fish. The grill really helps to keep it all together. Sole easily absorbs the teriyaki flavor. Pictured on page 36.

Commercial thick teriyaki sauce	$^1/_3$ cup	75 mL
Freshly squeezed lemon juice	2 tbsp.	30 mL
Finely grated lemon peel	$^1/_2$ tsp.	2 mL
Sesame oil	1 tsp.	5 mL
Toasted sesame seeds	2 tbsp.	30 mL
Ground ginger	$^1/_4$ tsp.	1 mL
Sole fillets (about 5 oz., 140 g, each)	4	4
Green onions, cut into 4 inch (10 cm) lengths and slivered lengthwise	2	2
4 inch (10 cm) bamboo skewers, soaked in water for 10 minutes	4	4

Preheat lightly sprayed 2-sided electric grill for 5 minutes. Combine first 6 ingredients in small bowl. Pour into shallow oblong casserole. ■ Drag fish through marinade to coat both sides. ■ Lay $^1/_4$ of green onion slivers crosswise along length of each fillet. Roll up each fillet tightly, enclosing onion. Cut each fillet in half crosswise. Slide 2 pieces onto each skewer to hold ends closed. Brush remaining marinade on fish rolls. Place on grill. Close lid. Cook for 5 minutes. Makes 4 skewers.

1 skewer: 211 Calories; 5.6 g Total Fat; 564 mg Sodium; 34 g Protein; 5 g Carbohydrate; 1 g Dietary Fiber

Sea Bass à la Caesar

If you have never had sea bass, this is a must-try recipe. Absolutely wonderful. Pictured on page 17.

Creamy Caesar dressing	2 tbsp.	30 mL
Lemon juice	2 tsp.	10 mL
Garlic cloves, minced	2	2
Fresh (or frozen) sea bass steaks (about 6 oz., 170 g, each)	2	2
Freshly ground pepper, generous sprinkle		
Fresh oregano leaves (or marjoram sprigs), to cover surface of fish		

(continued on next page)

Preheat lightly sprayed 2-sided electric grill for 5 minutes. Combine dressing, lemon juice and garlic in small bowl. ■ Spread over top surface of fish steaks. ■ Sprinkle with pepper. Lay oregano leaves over top.

For frozen fish: Place fish on grill. Close lid. Cook for 10 minutes until fish flakes easily with fork near bone.

For fresh or thawed fish: Place fish on grill. Close lid. Cook for 6 to 8 minutes until fish flakes easily with fork near bone.

Serves 2.

1 serving: 273 Calories; 13.6 g Total Fat; 213 mg Sodium; 32 g Protein; 3 g Carbohydrate; trace Dietary Fiber

Lemon Seafood

Serve with couscous, pasta or rice as an entrée, or arrange on a bed of lettuce with decorative picks as a predinner appetizer.

White (or alcohol-free white) wine	**1 tbsp.**	**15 mL**
Lemon juice	**2 tsp.**	**10 mL**
Garlic clove, minced	**1**	**1**
Chopped green onion	**2 tbsp.**	**30 mL**
Chopped fresh parsley	**1 tbsp.**	**15 mL**
Seasoned salt	**1/2 tsp.**	**2 mL**
Freshly ground pepper, sprinkle		
Medium frozen deveined raw shrimp, peeled	**1/2 lb.**	**225 g**
Medium frozen scallops	**1/2 lb.**	**225 g**

Preheat lightly sprayed 2-sided electric grill for 5 minutes. Combine first 7 ingredients in medium bowl. ■ Add frozen seafood and toss together to distribute green onion and parsley. Turn out contents of bowl onto grill. Close lid. Cook for 8 minutes. Scallops should be opaque and shrimp should be curled and pink. Discard liquids in drip tray. Serves 4.

1 serving: 115 Calories; 1.4 g Total Fat; 345 mg Sodium; 21 g Protein; 3 g Carbohydrate; trace Dietary Fiber

Grilled Pepper And Tomato Sandwiches

A very creamy but crisp veggie sandwich. Pictured on page 36.

Focaccia bread	1	1
Light (or non-fat) spreadable cream cheese	6 tbsp.	100 mL
Green pepper slivers	6 tbsp.	100 mL
Thick tomato slices	9	9
Garlic cloves, minced	3	3
Chopped fresh sweet basil	3 tbsp.	50 mL
Chopped fresh oregano leaves	3 tbsp.	50 mL
Salt	1 tsp.	5 mL
Pepper	$1/4$ tsp.	1 mL
Grated part-skim mozzarella cheese	1 cup	250 mL

Preheat lightly sprayed 2-sided electric grill for 5 minutes. Split focaccia bread in half horizontally. Spread each cut side with thin layer of cream cheese. ■ Place green pepper slivers and tomato slices on grill. Sprinkle garlic, basil, oregano, salt and pepper over vegetables. Close lid. Cook for 2 to 3 minutes until green pepper is tender-crisp. ■ Sprinkle cheese on top of vegetables. Close lid. Cook for 30 seconds to 1 minute, just to melt cheese. Carefully lift off and place on bottom half of focaccia. Cover with top half. Cut into 8 wedges. Place 2 wedges on grill. Close lid. Heat for about 2 minutes. Repeat with remaining wedges. Makes 8 sandwiches.

1 sandwich: 226 Calories; 4.9 g Total Fat; 803 mg Sodium; 10 g Protein; 35 g Carbohydrate; 1 g Dietary Fiber

Variation: Use 6 tbsp. (100 mL) mayonnaise, salad dressing or Caesar dressing in place of cream cheese.

Sweet-Filled Apples

Serve with ice cream or whipping cream to complete this dessert. Pictured on page 72.

Brown sugar, packed	2 tbsp.	30 mL
Chopped pecans	1 tbsp.	15 mL
Rolled oats (not instant)	1 tbsp.	15 mL
Ground cinnamon	$1/4$ tsp.	1 mL
Hard margarine (or butter)	1 tbsp.	15 mL
Medium red apples, with peel	4	4
Lemon juice	1 tbsp.	15 mL

(continued on next page)

Preheat lightly sprayed 2-sided electric grill for 5 minutes. Measure first 5 ingredients into small bowl. Mash with fork until crumbly. Makes about 6 tbsp. (100 mL) filling. ■ Cut apples in half lengthwise. Remove core with melon baller or knife. Brush cut sides of apples with lemon juice. Place 2 apple halves on grill. Close lid. Cook for 5 minutes. Fill each cavity with about 2 packed tsp. (10 mL) brown sugar mixture. Close lid. Cook for 6 to 8 minutes until sugar mixture is melted and apple is soft. Repeat with remaining apple halves and brown sugar mixture. Makes 8 apple halves.

1 apple half: 76 Calories; 2.4 g Total Fat; 21 mg Sodium; trace Protein; 15 g Carbohydrate; 1 g Dietary Fiber

Fruity Streusel Toast

Serve with maple syrup if desired. Pictured on page 89.

Large eggs	**4**	**4**
Milk	**¹/₄ cup**	**60 mL**
Salt	**¹/₄ tsp.**	**1 mL**
Vanilla	**1 tsp.**	**5 mL**
Thick whole wheat (or white) bread slices (such as Texas toast style)	**4**	**4**
Diced fresh fruit or whole berries	**¹/₂ cup**	**125 mL**
Brown sugar, packed	**2 tbsp.**	**30 mL**
All-purpose flour	**1 tbsp.**	**15 mL**
Rolled oats (not instant)	**1 tbsp.**	**15 mL**
Ground cinnamon	**¹/₁₆ tsp.**	**0.5 mL**
Hard margarine (or butter), cut up	**1 tbsp.**	**15 mL**

Preheat lightly sprayed 2-sided electric grill for 5 minutes. Whisk first 4 ingredients together in shallow pan. Soak bread slices in egg mixture for about 2 minutes on each side until liquid is absorbed. ■ Scatter fruit over 2 soaked bread slices. Cover with remaining 2 soaked bread slices. ■ Combine brown sugar, flour, rolled oats and cinnamon in small bowl. Mash in margarine with fork until mixture is crumbly. Sprinkle on top bread slices. Carefully place both sandwiches on grill. Close lid. Cook for 5 minutes. Makes 2 sandwiches.

1 sandwich: 658 Calories; 19.5 g Total Fat; 1156 mg Sodium; 26 g Protein; 100 g Carbohydrate; 9 g Dietary Fiber

Reuben Supper

Great combination for a full-meal presentation. Serve with a grainy mustard.

Pork sausage meat	**1 lb.**	**454 g**
Swiss cheese, thinly sliced	**2 oz.**	**57 g**
Sauerkraut, drained	**1 cup**	**250 mL**
Chopped onion	**$^1/_2$ cup**	**125 mL**
Thin potato slices	**2 cups**	**500 mL**
Salt, sprinkle		
Pepper, sprinkle		

Preheat lightly sprayed 2-sided electric grill for 5 minutes. Form sausage meat into 1 flattened patty about size of grill. ■ Place patty on grill. Cover sausage patty with cheese, sauerkraut and onion. Top with potato slices. Sprinkle with salt and pepper. Close lid. Cook for 15 minutes until browned and potato is soft. Serves 4.

1 serving: 343 Calories; 23.4 g Total Fat; 760 mg Sodium; 14 g Protein; 20 g Carbohydrate; 3 g Dietary Fiber

Fast Chili

For a spicier version try the variation with salsa listed below. Serve over noodles.

Lean ground beef	**1 lb.**	**454 g**
Chili powder	**2 tsp.**	**10 mL**
Salt	**$^1/_4$ tsp.**	**1 mL**
Freshly ground pepper, generous sprinkle		
Canned red kidney beans, drained and rinsed	**14 oz.**	**398 mL**
Tomato sauce	**$7^1/_2$ oz.**	**213 mL**
Chopped tomato	**$^1/_2$ cup**	**125 mL**
Chopped green pepper	**$^1/_3$ cup**	**75 mL**
Chopped onion	**$^1/_2$ cup**	**125 mL**
Garlic clove, minced	**1**	**1**

(continued on next page)

Preheat lightly sprayed 2-sided electric grill for 5 minutes. Crumble ground beef over bottom of grill. Sprinkle with about $^1/_2$ of amounts of chili powder, salt and pepper. Scatter kidney beans over beef and season again with remaining amounts of chili powder, salt and pepper. Pour $^1/_2$ of tomato sauce over. ■ Combine remaining 4 ingredients in small bowl with remaining $^1/_2$ of tomato sauce. Pour over kidney beans and beef. Close lid. Cook for 7 to 8 minutes until beef is no longer pink and vegetables are tender. Makes 4 cups (1 L).

1 cup (250 mL): 279 Calories; 10.1 g Total Fat; 696 mg Sodium; 27 g Protein; 21 g Carbohydrate;
    6 g Dietary Fiber

Variation: Substitute spicy salsa for tomato sauce for more "kick."

Potato Pancakes

Garnish with sour cream or applesauce. Delicious with either one! Pictured on page 125.

Frozen shredded hash brown potatoes, partially thawed	**4 cups**	**1 L**
Chopped green onion	**$^3/_4$ cup**	**175 mL**
Large eggs, fork-beaten	**2**	**2**
All-purpose flour	**$^1/_4$ cup**	**60 mL**
Baking powder	**1 tsp.**	**5 mL**
Salt	**1 tsp.**	**5 mL**
Pepper	**$^1/_4$ tsp.**	**1 mL**

Preheat lightly sprayed 2-sided electric grill for 5 minutes. Combine all 7 ingredients in medium bowl. Spoon potato mixture onto grill in 2 portions. Close lid. Cook for 13 minutes. Makes 2 large pancakes, enough for 4 servings.

$^1/_2$ pancake (1 serving): 258 Calories; 4 g Total Fat; 1832 mg Sodium; 9 g Protein; 48 g Carbohydrate;
    5 g Dietary Fiber

· ·

To ensure that food will not overcook, and for safety reasons, keep oven mitts and pot holders in clear sight near the outdoor barbecue for those unpredictable flare-ups.

Warm Penne And Vegetables

Lots of slicing and dicing but the flavor is well worth the effort! Pictured on page 126.

Water	1/2 cup	125 mL
Vegetable bouillon powder	2 tsp.	10 mL
White (or alcohol-free white) wine	1/4 cup	60 mL
Cornstarch	1 1/2 tsp.	7 mL
Chopped fresh sweet basil	4 tbsp.	60 mL
Chopped fresh oregano leaves	2 tbsp.	30 mL
Freshly ground pepper, generous sprinkle		
Japanese eggplant, about 2 inches (5 cm) in diameter and 12 inches (30 cm) long, halved lengthwise	1	1
Medium zucchini (about 12 inches, 30 cm, long), peeled and cut in half lengthwise	1	1
Portabello mushroom, black "gills" scraped off with spoon	1	1
Medium red onion, halved crosswise	1	1
Minced garlic	1 tbsp.	15 mL
Medium yellow pepper, halved and seeded	1	1
Roma (plum) tomatoes, halved crosswise	4	4
Penne pasta (about 6 oz., 170 g)	1 1/2 cups	375 mL
Boiling water	2 1/2 qts.	2.5 L
Salt	2 tsp.	10 mL
Grated part-skim mozzarella cheese	1/2 cup	125 mL
Grated Parmesan cheese	1/4 cup	60 mL

Preheat lightly sprayed 2-sided electric grill for 5 minutes. Combine first 4 ingredients in small saucepan. Bring to a boil. Boil for about 3 minutes. ■ Add basil, oregano and pepper. Stir. Remove from heat. ■ Arrange eggplant, zucchini, mushroom and red onion on grill. Sprinkle with garlic. Close lid. Cook for 8 minutes. Remove to cutting board. Dice and place in large bowl. ■ Repeat with yellow pepper and tomato, but cook only for 5 minutes. Any collected juices in drip tray should be poured over vegetables in bowl. Pour herb and wine sauce over vegetables. Toss to coat. ■ Cook penne in boiling water and salt in large pot or Dutch oven for 10 to 12 minutes until just tender. Drain. Add to vegetables. Toss. ■ Add both cheeses. Toss until well combined and most liquid is absorbed. Serves 4.

1 serving: 282 Calories; 5.9 g Total Fat; 513 mg Sodium; 15 g Protein; 42 g Carbohydrate; 5 g Dietary Fiber

Vegetables

ake advantage of garden markets during the spring and summer months to pick up all your favorite vegetables in their freshest state. Vegetable flavors are sharp and texture is crisp when grilled—so little nutrition is lost. The added cost of buying at the garden market can be offset by serving smaller portions of meat and planning two or three different vegetables.

Acorn And Apple

Wonderful served with pork roast or ham steaks.

Tub margarine	1 tbsp.	15 mL
Acorn squash, cut into quarters lengthwise and seeds removed	1	1
Chopped onion	$^1/_3$ cup	75 mL
Chopped celery	$^1/_3$ cup	75 mL
Diced red apple, with peel	$1^1/_2$ cups	375 mL
Brown sugar, packed	1 tbsp.	15 mL
Ground cardamom	$^1/_4$ tsp.	1 mL
Ground cinnamon	$^1/_4$ tsp.	1 mL
Salt	$^1/_8$ tsp.	0.5 mL
Toasted chopped pecans	2 tsp.	10 mL

Preheat barbecue to medium. Melt margarine in non-stick skillet over medium. Brush some of margarine onto cut surface of squash. ■ Sauté onion and celery in remaining margarine in skillet until soft. ■ Add apple. Cook for 2 minutes. ■ Sprinkle with brown sugar, cardamom, cinnamon and salt. Stir well. Place squash, cut side down, on greased grill. Cook for about 15 minutes. Turn, cut side up. Fill cavities with apple mixture. Close lid. Cook for 20 to 30 minutes until squash is tender. ■ Sprinkle with pecans. Serves 4.

1 serving: 120 Calories; 4.2 g Total Fat; 142 mg Sodium; 2 g Protein; 22 g Carbohydrate; 3 g Dietary Fiber

Cheese-Stuffed Tomatoes

Yummy stuffed tomato with melted cheese and crunchy buttered bread crumbs.

Medium firm tomatoes	2	2
Dried sweet basil (or dried whole oregano), crushed	$^1/_8$ tsp.	0.5 mL
Salt, sprinkle		
Freshly ground pepper, sprinkle		
Grated part-skim mozzarella cheese	$^2/_3$ cup	150 mL
Fine dry bread crumbs	$^1/_4$ cup	60 mL
Tub margarine, melted	4 tsp.	20 mL
Grated Parmesan (or Romano) cheese	2 tsp.	10 mL

Preheat lightly sprayed electric grill to medium-high. Cut tomatoes in half crosswise. Remove seeds and juice from between ribs. Sprinkle each half with basil, salt and pepper. ■ Pack cavities with mozzarella cheese. ■ Combine bread crumbs, melted margarine and Parmesan cheese in small bowl. Spoon over tops of both tomatoes. Place, crumb side up, on grill. Cook for 12 to 15 minutes until cheese is melted and tomato is soft. Makes 4 stuffed tomato halves.

1 stuffed tomato half: 132 Calories; 7.9 g Total Fat; 224 mg Sodium; 7 g Protein; 9 g Carbohydrate; 1 g Dietary Fiber

Grilled Tomatoes

The appealing flavors of garlic and basil complement the grilled tomatoes. Pictured on page 143.

Medium firm tomatoes	4	4
Olive oil	1 tbsp.	15 mL
Garlic clove, minced	1	1
Salt	$^1/_4$-$^1/_2$ tsp.	1-2 mL
Freshly ground pepper, sprinkle		
Large fresh sweet basil leaves, stacked, rolled tightly lengthwise, then cut crosswise into very thin slivers (chiffonade)	2 tbsp.	30 mL
Grated Parmesan cheese	1 tbsp.	15 mL

(continued on next page)

Preheat lightly sprayed electric grill to high. Cut tomatoes in half crosswise. Remove seeds and juice from between ribs. ■ Combine olive oil and garlic in small dish. Brush cut tomato surfaces generously with oil mixture until used up. ■ Sprinkle each half with salt and pepper. Place, cut side down, on grill. Cook for 2 minutes. Turn, cut side up. ■ Sprinkle with basil and cheese. Cook for 2 minutes. Makes 8 tomato halves.

1 tomato half: 32 Calories; 2.2 g Total Fat; 105 mg Sodium; 1 g Protein; 3 g Carbohydrate; 1 g Dietary Fiber

Marinated Grilled Eggplant

An outstanding way to serve eggplant.

Small eggplants	**2**	**2**
Salt	**2 tsp.**	**10 mL**
Olive oil	**2 tbsp.**	**30 mL**
Olive oil	**1/4 cup**	**60 mL**
Red wine vinegar	**1/4 cup**	**60 mL**
Apple juice	**1/4 cup**	**60 mL**
Garlic cloves, minced	**3**	**3**
Anchovy paste	**1/2 tbsp.**	**7 mL**
Green onion, thinly sliced	**1**	**1**
Drained capers	**2 tbsp.**	**30 mL**
Chopped fresh parsley	**1/4 cup**	**60 mL**
Salt	**1/4 tsp.**	**1 mL**
Freshly ground pepper, sprinkle		

Cut ends off eggplants. Cut 1/4 inch (6 mm) lengthwise slices of unpeeled eggplant. Sprinkle 1 side of each slice very lightly with first amount of salt. Place in colander for 30 minutes to drain released juices. Rinse each slice and pat dry with paper towel. Preheat lightly sprayed electric grill to medium-high. Brush each side of slices with first amount of olive oil. Cook for 3 minutes per side until tender. As slices cook, remove from grill and roll up tightly. Secure with wooden pick. Place in single layer in shallow baking dish. ■ Combine remaining 10 ingredients in small bowl. Makes about 1 cup (250 mL) marinade. Pour over eggplant. Cover. Marinate in refrigerator for at least 5 hours, turning rolls several times. Bring to room temperature to serve. Drain and discard marinade. Makes about 20 rolls. Serves 8.

1 serving: 74 Calories; 7.1 g Total Fat; 240 mg Sodium; 1 g Protein; 3 g Carbohydrate; 1 g Dietary Fiber

Eggplant Stacks

If you've never tried eggplant, these stacks will have you wanting more!

Medium eggplant, unpeeled and sliced crosswise into $^1/_2$ inch (12 mm) rounds	1	1
Salt	$^3/_4$ **tsp.**	**4 mL**
Olive oil	$^1/_4$ **cup**	**60 mL**
Garlic clove, minced	1	1
Large tomatoes, sliced	2	2
Large fresh sweet basil leaves, stacked, rolled tightly lengthwise, then cut crosswise into very thin slivers (chiffonade)	5	5
Grated Parmesan cheese	**4 tsp.**	**20 mL**

Sprinkle eggplant slices on both sides with salt. Lay on paper towels and let stand for 30 minutes. Dab top side with more paper towel, lightly pressing each slice to remove more moisture. ■ Preheat lightly sprayed electric grill to high. Combine olive oil and garlic. Brush lightly on both sides of eggplant. Cook slices for 10 to 14 minutes, turning frequently, until almost tender when poked with fork. ■ Lay 1 tomato slice on each eggplant slice. Brush lightly with oil mixture. ■ Sprinkle basil over tomato. Sprinkle cheese over basil. Cook on grill for 2 to 3 minutes until tomato is warmed and eggplant is tender. Makes about 8 stacks.

1 stack: 85 Calories; 7.7 g Total Fat; 150 mg Sodium; 1 g Protein; 4 g Carbohydrate; 1 g Dietary Fiber

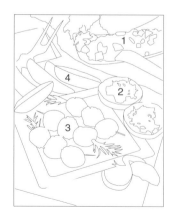

1. Sweet Grilled Salsa, page 13
2. Grilled Tomatoes, page 140
3. Rosemary Scallops, page 114
4. Crispy Potato Wedges, page 148

Italian Mushroom Grill

Tastes like "bruschetta" in a mushroom. Excellent. Pictured on front cover.

Water	¹/₃ **cup**	**75 mL**
Balsamic vinegar	**2 tbsp.**	**30 mL**
Garlic clove, minced	**1**	**1**
Dried sweet basil	**1 tsp.**	**5 mL**
Dried whole oregano	¹/₂ **tsp.**	**2 mL**
Salt, sprinkle		
Freshly ground pepper, sprinkle		
Portabello mushrooms, large and nicely shaped	**4**	**4**
Olive oil	**4 tsp.**	**20 mL**
Small roma (plum) tomatoes, seeded and chopped	**2**	**2**
Sliced green onion	¹/₄ **cup**	**60 mL**
Grated Parmesan cheese	¹/₄ **cup**	**60 mL**

Combine first 7 ingredients in small bowl. Makes 6 tbsp. (100 mL) marinade. ■ Remove stems from mushrooms and reserve for another purpose. Scrape and discard black "gills" from around underside of mushrooms with spoon. Place mushrooms in shallow casserole. Pour marinade over mushrooms. Marinate at room temperature for 30 minutes, turning over several times. ■ Preheat lightly sprayed electric grill to high. Drain and reserve marinade for basting. Brush inside of mushrooms with some of olive oil. Place, oiled side down, on grill. Brush other side of mushrooms with remaining olive oil. Cook for 10 minutes, turning and basting surfaces with reserved marinade several times. ■ Remove to broiler pan. Discard any remaining marinade. Pile inside of mushrooms with tomato, green onion and cheese. Broil in oven for 2 to 3 minutes until cheese is melted and tomato is warm. Serves 4.

1 serving: 127 Calories; 7.4 g Total Fat; 137 mg Sodium; 7 g Protein; 12 g Carbohydrate; 3 g Dietary Fiber

1. Grilled Pepper Medley, page 151
2. Hazelnut Halibut, page 114

Santa Fe Mushroom

This recipe easily multiplies to your number of guests. There's plenty of room on the barbecue for more.

Salsa (mild or medium)	**¹/₃ cup**	**75 mL**
Garlic clove, minced	**1**	**1**
Chili powder	**¹/₂ tsp.**	**2 mL**
Ground cumin	**¹/₄ tsp.**	**1 mL**
Portabello mushroom, large and nicely shaped	**1**	**1**
Canola oil	**1 tsp.**	**5 mL**

Combine first 4 ingredients in blender. Process until smooth. Makes ¹/₃ cup (75 mL) marinade. ■ Remove stem from mushroom and reserve for another purpose. Scrape and discard black "gills" from around underside of mushroom with spoon. Pour marinade over mushroom. Marinate at room temperature for 30 minutes, turning several times. ■ Preheat barbecue to medium-high. Remove mushroom and reserve marinade for basting. Brush mushroom inside and out with oil. Cook on greased grill for 5 to 6 minutes, turning and basting surface with reserved marinade several times, until tender. Discard any remaining marinade. Serves 1.

1 serving: 134 Calories; 5.6 g Total Fat; 1312 mg Sodium; 5 g Protein; 20 g Carbohydrate; 4 g Dietary Fiber

Grilled Asparagus

Make these pretty bundles when asparagus is young and tender. Pictured on front cover.

Olive oil	**1 tbsp.**	**15 mL**
Garlic clove, minced	**1**	**1**
Lemon pepper, sprinkle		
Fresh asparagus spears, trimmed	**1 lb.**	**454 g**
Boiling water	**2 cups**	**500 mL**
Long chives, for tying		
Prepared orange juice	**2 tbsp.**	**30 mL**

(continued on next page)

Preheat lightly sprayed electric grill to medium-high. Combine olive oil, garlic and lemon pepper in small bowl. ■ Lay asparagus in boiling water in large saucepan. Cover. Simmer gently for 3 minutes until bright green. Immediately plunge into ice water to cool. ■ Tie bundles of 3 spears around middle with chives. Place bundles on grill. Baste with olive oil mixture. Cook for 10 minutes, turning and basting several times, until tender-crisp. ■ Remove bundles to shallow serving dish. Drizzle orange juice over asparagus. Serves 4.

1 serving: 60 Calories; 3.7 g Total Fat; 2 mg Sodium; 4 g Protein; 5 g Carbohydrate; 2 g Dietary Fiber

Grilled Onion Slices

Spicy, sweet onions are delicious served over barbecued steak or separately as a vegetable.

Large sweet onions (such as Vidalia, Walla Walla or Maui)	**3**	**3**
Chili sauce	**1/4 cup**	**60 mL**
Olive oil	**2 tbsp.**	**30 mL**
Liquid honey	**2 tsp.**	**10 mL**
Chili powder	**1/2 tsp.**	**2 mL**
Cayenne pepper	**1/8 tsp.**	**0.5 mL**

Preheat lightly sprayed electric grill to high. Cut onions into crosswise slices, 1/2 inch (12 mm) thick. Place on grill. Cook for 2 minutes per side. ■ Combine remaining 5 ingredients in small bowl. Makes 6 tbsp. (100 mL) basting sauce. Brush onion slices with sauce. Cook for 3 to 4 minutes per side, turning and basting several times, until soft and browned. Discard any remaining sauce. Makes about 12 slices.

1 slice: 38 Calories; 2.1 g Total Fat; 75 mg Sodium; trace Protein; 5 g Carbohydrate; 1 g Dietary Fiber

•••••••••••••••••••••••••••••••

Veggie Packets - Clean and prepare fresh vegetables as desired. Place on a sheet of heavy-duty foil (or double thickness of regular foil) that has been lightly sprayed. Top veggies with a dab of butter or margarine, a bit of water (or an ice cube) and a sprinkle of seasonings. Close up foil with double folds, leaving room for slight steam expansion.

Crispy Potato Wedges

Give your meals a boost with these spicy little gems. Pictured on page 143.

Medium Russet potatoes, scrubbed and cut lengthwise into quarters	4	4
Boiling water, to cover		
Salt	1 tsp.	5 mL
Garlic salt	1 tsp.	5 mL
Freshly ground pepper	1 tsp.	5 mL
Ground cumin	1 tsp.	5 mL
Paprika	1 tsp.	5 mL
Cayenne pepper	¹/₂ tsp.	2 mL
Olive oil	4 tsp.	20 mL

Par-boil potatoes in boiling water and salt in medium saucepan for 5 minutes. Drain. Return saucepan to still hot burner and shake back and forth to dry potatoes slightly. ■ Combine next 5 ingredients in small bowl. ■ Preheat lightly sprayed electric grill to high. Put potatoes into large bowl. Drizzle with olive oil. Toss well to coat evenly. Sprinkle seasoning mixture over potatoes while tossing, until well distributed. Place potatoes on grill. Cook for about 20 minutes, turning frequently, until potatoes are tender and crispy brown. Serves 4.

1 serving: 175 Calories; 5 g Total Fat; 178 mg Sodium; 3 g Protein; 31 g Carbohydrate; 3 g Dietary Fiber

Sweet Sweet Potatoes

These sweet potatoes are even tastier with the added brown sugar.

Medium sweet potatoes, scrubbed and cut on diagonal into ¹/₂ inch (12 mm) slices	2	2
Tub margarine, melted	3 tbsp.	50 mL
Brown sugar, packed	¹/₃ cup	75 mL

Preheat lightly sprayed electric grill to high. Brush 1 cut side of each slice of sweet potato with melted margarine. Place, buttered side down, on hot grill. Brush upper side with melted margarine. Cook for 5 minutes. Turn slices over. ■ Sprinkle with about 1 tsp. (5 mL) brown sugar per slice. Cook for 5 to 6 minutes until slices are tender and sugar is caramelized. Makes about 16 slices.

1 slice: 49 Calories; 2 g Total Fat; 30 mg Sodium; trace Protein; 8 g Carbohydrate; trace Dietary Fiber

Stuffed Peppers

This makes a delicious and attractive side dish with any entrée. Pictured on page 90.

Wild rice	¹/₂ **cup**	**125 mL**
Boiling water	2¹/₂ **cups**	**625 mL**
Salt	**1 tsp.**	**5 mL**
Brown rice	¹/₂ **cup**	**125 mL**
Chopped onion	¹/₂ **cup**	**125 mL**
Garlic clove, minced	**1**	**1**
Pine nuts, chopped	**2 tbsp.**	**30 mL**
Olive oil	**1 tbsp.**	**15 mL**
Small tomato, seeded and diced small	**1**	**1**
Chopped fresh parsley	**3 tbsp.**	**50 mL**
Salt	¹/₂ **tsp.**	**2 mL**
Freshly ground pepper, sprinkle		
Small red, orange or yellow peppers	**3**	**3**
Olive oil	**1 tbsp.**	**15 mL**
Freshly ground pepper, for garnish		
Chopped fresh parsley, for garnish		

Measure wild rice into boiling water and first amount of salt in large saucepan. Simmer, covered, for 10 minutes. Stir in brown rice. Simmer, covered, for 40 minutes until rice is cooked and water is absorbed. ■ Sauté onion, garlic and pine nuts in first amount of olive oil in large non-stick skillet for 5 minutes until onion is soft. ■ Stir in tomato, cooked rice, parsley, second amount of salt and pepper. Makes about 3 cups (750 mL) stuffing. ■ Preheat lightly sprayed electric grill to medium. Split peppers in half lengthwise through stem. Discard seeds and membrane. Brush pepper halves inside and out with second amount of olive oil. Place, cut side down, on grill. Cook for 1 minute. Turn peppers over. Cook for about 15 minutes. Divide stuffing among pepper halves. Cook on grill for 15 minutes until rice is heated through and pepper halves are tender-crisp. Sprinkle with pepper and parsley. Makes 6 stuffed pepper halves.

1 stuffed pepper half: 189 Calories; 7.1 g Total Fat; 684 mg Sodium; 5 g Protein; 28 g Carbohydrate; 3 g Dietary Fiber

Grilled Peperonata

Can be served as a side dish or tossed with pasta. The tangy balsamic vegetables are good either way. Pictured on page 125.

Olive oil	3 tbsp.	50 mL
Garlic cloves, minced	2	2
Fresh rosemary leaves, chopped	2 tsp.	10 mL
Medium green pepper, halved and seeded	1	1
Medium red pepper, halved and seeded	1	1
Medium orange pepper, halved and seeded	1	1
Medium yellow pepper, halved and seeded	1	1
Large red onion, peeled and thickly sliced	1	1
Balsamic vinegar, to taste	2 tbsp.-$^1/_4$ cup	30-60 mL
Chopped fresh parsley	1 tbsp.	15 mL

Combine olive oil, garlic and rosemary in small bowl. Let stand at room temperature for 30 minutes to meld flavors. ■ Preheat lightly sprayed electric grill to high. Brush peppers and red onion with some of oil mixture. Cook on grill for 6 to 8 minutes, turning and brushing with oil mixture several times, until vegetables are tender-crisp. Remove vegetables to cutting board. Dice into $^3/_4$ inch (2 cm) pieces. Remove to large bowl. ■ Toss peppers and red onion with vinegar. Toss with parsley. Makes about 6 cups (1.5 L).

$^1/_2$ cup (125 mL): 43 Calories; 3.5 g Total Fat; 1 mg Sodium; trace Protein; 3 g Carbohydrate; 1 g Dietary Fiber

If your outdoor barbecue is charcoal, or is gas without a gauge or with a faulty one, try this: Place your hand, palm-side down, no less than eight inches directly above the heat source. Keep your hand there, counting the seconds, until the heat is uncomfortable and you automatically pull your hand away. If you can hold your hand in for 5 seconds, the temperature is low; for 4 seconds, the temperature is medium; for 3 seconds, it is medium-high; and for 2 seconds - it's hot!

Grilled Pepper Medley

Peppers take some time to grill. Patience will be rewarded by the wonderful flavor. Pictured on page 144 and back cover.

Olive oil	3 tbsp.	50 mL
Balsamic vinegar	1/4 cup	60 mL
GRILLED PEPPERS		
Medium green pepper, quartered and seeded lengthwise	1	1
Medium red pepper, quartered and seeded lengthwise	1	1
Medium orange pepper, quartered and seeded lengthwise	1	1
Medium yellow pepper, quartered and seeded lengthwise	1	1
Chopped green onion	1/4 cup	60 mL
Chopped fresh cilantro (or fresh mint leaves)	1/4 cup	60 mL
Canned sliced ripe olives, drained	4 1/2 oz.	125 mL

Combine olive oil and vinegar in small bowl. ■ **Grilled Peppers:** Preheat lightly sprayed electric grill to high. Brush inside of pepper pieces with some of vinaigrette. Reserve remainder. Place peppers, cut side down, on grill. Cook for 2 minutes. Turn skin side down. Cook for 15 minutes until peppers are soft and skins are charred and blistered in places. Place pepper pieces in bowl. Cover with plastic wrap. Let sweat for about 15 minutes until cool enough to handle. Remove and discard skin from peppers by scraping with knife. Dice peppers into about 3/4 inch (2 cm) pieces.
■ Combine peppers, green onion, cilantro and olives in medium bowl. Toss with reserved vinaigrette. Let stand at room temperature for 30 minutes to meld flavors. Makes about 3 cups (750 mL).

1/2 cup (125 mL): 86 Calories; 7.8 g Total Fat; 66 mg Sodium; 1 g Protein; 5 g Carbohydrate; 1 g Dietary Fiber

To make your own drip pan, use a large square of heavy-duty foil. Fold all four edges over twice, about 1 1/2 inches (3.8 cm) each time. Take folded portions and bend up at right angles to bottom, forming sides. Miter corners to reinforce.

Italian Zucchini

One of the tastiest ways to enjoy zucchini.

Olive oil	2 tbsp.	30 mL
Balsamic vinegar	2 tbsp.	30 mL
Small garlic clove, minced	1	1
Salt	1/2 tsp.	2 mL
Freshly ground pepper, sprinkle		
Dried whole oregano, crushed	1/4 tsp.	1 mL
Dried sweet basil, crushed	1/4 tsp.	1 mL
Small zucchini (about 6 inches, 15 cm, long), with peel, cut on sharp diagonal to make 4 pieces each (for a total of 16)	4	4

Whisk first 7 ingredients together in large container with lid. Makes 1/4 cup (60 mL) marinade. ■ Add zucchini pieces. Toss well to coat. Marinate at room temperature for 30 minutes, tossing frequently. Preheat lightly sprayed electric grill to high. Remove zucchini, reserving marinade for basting. Place zucchini on grill. Cook for 5 to 6 minutes per side, basting with remaining marinade. Serves 4.

1 serving: 83 Calories; 7.1 g Total Fat; 344 mg Sodium; 2 g Protein; 5 g Carbohydrate; 2 g Dietary Fiber

Corn On The Cob On The BBQ

Leave "stalk" to use as handle for eating. Recipe can easily be doubled or tripled. Spread hot cobs with butter, or better yet, Herbed Butter, page 22, or Spanish Butter, page 153, and salt and pepper.

Cobs of corn, with husk and silk left on	2	2
Cold water, to cover		

Do not remove husk or silk from corn. Soak cobs in cold water for 30 minutes. Preheat barbecue to low. Place cobs on ungreased grill. Close lid. Cook for about 30 minutes, turning every 10 minutes, until kernels are tender. Let stand in husks for about 15 minutes until cool enough to handle. Pull back husks. Pull off silk. Serves 2.

1 serving: 194 Calories; 2.3 g Total Fat; 31 mg Sodium; 6 g Protein; 45 g Carbohydrate; 7 g Dietary Fiber

Spanish Corn

Kind of a different flavor for corn on the cob.

SPANISH BUTTER		
Capers, drained	**3**	**3**
Pimiento-stuffed green olives	**2**	**2**
Butter (or hard margarine), softened	**1 tbsp.**	**15 mL**
Small garlic clove, minced	**1**	**1**
Cayenne pepper, sprinkle		
Freshly ground pepper, sprinkle		
Cob of corn, with husk	**1**	**1**

Spanish Butter: Preheat barbecue to medium. Combine capers and olives in small bowl, mashing with fork until in small bits. ■ Add butter, garlic, cayenne pepper and pepper. Mix well. ■ Remove large outer husks from corn and discard. Peel back inner husks without removing completely. Remove and discard silk. Spread cob with butter mixture. Pull up husk around cob. Tie in 3 places with butcher's string to secure. Place cob on ungreased grill. Close lid. Cook for about 30 minutes, turning every 10 minutes, until corn is tender. Remove string and husks to serve. Serves 1.

1 serving: 381 Calories; 22.6 g Total Fat; 1782 mg Sodium; 7 g Protein; 47 g Carbohydrate; 10 g Dietary Fiber

Measurement Tables

Throughout this book measurements are given in Conventional and Metric measure. To compensate for differences between the two measurements due to rounding, a full metric measure is not always used. The cup used is the standard 8 fluid ounce. Temperature is given in degrees Fahrenheit and Celsius. Baking pan measurements are in inches and centimetres as well as quarts and litres. An exact metric conversion is given below as well as the working equivalent (Standard Measure).

OVEN TEMPERATURES

Fahrenheit (°F)	Celsius (°C)
175°	80°
200°	95°
225°	110°
250°	120°
275°	140°
300°	150°
325°	160°
350°	175°
375°	190°
400°	205°
425°	220°
450°	230°
475°	240°
500°	260°

SPOONS

Conventional Measure	Metric Exact Conversion Millilitre (mL)	Metric Standard Measure Millilitre (mL)
1/8 teaspoon (tsp.)	0.6 mL	0.5 mL
1/4 teaspoon (tsp.)	1.2 mL	1 mL
1/2 teaspoon (tsp.)	2.4 mL	2 mL
1 teaspoon (tsp.)	4.7 mL	5 mL
2 teaspoons (tsp.)	9.4 mL	10 mL
1 tablespoon (tbsp.)	14.2 mL	15 mL

CUPS

1/4 cup (4 tbsp.)	56.8 mL	60 mL
1/3 cup (5 1/3 tbsp.)	75.6 mL	75 mL
1/2 cup (8 tbsp.)	113.7 mL	125 mL
2/3 cup (10 2/3 tbsp.)	151.2 mL	150 mL
3/4 cup (12 tbsp.)	170.5 mL	175 mL
1 cup (16 tbsp.)	227.3 mL	250 mL
4 1/2 cups	1022.9 mL	1000 mL (1 L)

PANS

Conventional Inches	Metric Centimetres
8x8 inch	20x20 cm
9x9 inch	22x22 cm
9x13 inch	22x33 cm
10x15 inch	25x38 cm
11x17 inch	28x43 cm
8x2 inch round	20x5 cm
9x2 inch round	22x5 cm
10x4 1/2 inch tube	25x11 cm
8x4x3 inch loaf	20x10x7.5 cm
9x5x3 inch loaf	22x12.5x7.5 cm

DRY MEASUREMENTS

Conventional Measure Ounces (oz.)	Metric Exact Conversion Grams (g)	Metric Standard Measure Grams (g)
1 oz.	28.3 g	28 g
2 oz.	56.7 g	57 g
3 oz.	85.0 g	85 g
4 oz.	113.4 g	125 g
5 oz.	141.7 g	140 g
6 oz.	170.1 g	170 g
7 oz.	198.4 g	200 g
8 oz.	226.8 g	250 g
16 oz.	453.6 g	500 g
32 oz.	907.2 g	1000 g (1 kg)

CASSEROLES (Canada & Britain)

Standard Size Casserole	Exact Metric Measure
1 qt. (5 cups)	1.13 L
1 1/2 qts. (7 1/2 cups)	1.69 L
2 qts. (10 cups)	2.25 L
2 1/2 qts. (12 1/2 cups)	2.81 L
3 qts. (15 cups)	3.38 L
4 qts. (20 cups)	4.5 L
5 qts. (25 cups)	5.63 L

CASSEROLES (United States)

Standard Size Casserole	Exact Metric Measure
1 qt. (4 cups)	900 mL
1 1/2 qts. (6 cups)	1.35 L
2 qts. (8 cups)	1.8 L
2 1/2 qts. (10 cups)	2.25 L
3 qts. (12 cups)	2.7 L
4 qts. (16 cups)	3.6 L
5 qts. (20 cups)	4.5 L

Index